K

Dedication

This book is dedicated to Steve and Liz Crockford,
who introduced us to running
and whose friendship has been an inspiration.

Thanks to Phil Duffin for his work on the manuscript,
and to Steve Crockford for his illustrations.

Keep On Running

SUE BARNETT

KINGSWAY PUBLICATIONS
EASTBOURNE

ISBN 1 84291 026 4

Published by
KINGSWAY COMMUNICATIONS LTD
Lottbridge Drove, Eastbourne, BN23 6NT, England.
Email: books@kingsway.co.uk

Book design and production for the publishers by
Bookprint Creative Services, P.O. Box 827, BN21 3YJ, England.
Printed in Great Britain.

Contents

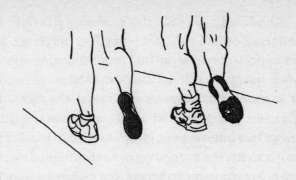

LAP 1

Run Around Sue

Every muscle in my body screamed out to stop. My bones ached for relief. My lungs were at bursting point, and my heart pounded with an urgent beat, demanding rest. A pathetic voice from within pleaded, 'You don't have to do this . . . give up! Quit!'

Gasps from the running thousands accompanied my deterioration. Others were collapsing, and the accumulative dejection was breaking me. No words adequately describe the mental and physical extremes of this human experience in a marathon. Up until twelve months before, I had been a 'short, sharp burster' – with nothing too uncomfortable, an end in view, and a team surrounding me, I could move faster than most to achieve the goal. In crippling contrast, my bruised, aching feet were now pounding the hard streets of London. There was no visible end in sight, no team around to support . . . just loneliness among the thousands. I had hit rock-bottom. I was fit to drop.

7

Never underestimate each day's running schedule. Office appointments, school runs, shopping lists, meetings: apparently unimportant events can lead to life-changing upheavals, and whole new perspectives! This was to hit me as I agreed to go for a seemingly harmless run round the block. I had recently met a young mum who had joined us at keep fit class, and one or two other events. Now I needed to join Liz in her choice of activity. The suggestion of a run intrigued me, partly because of her obvious excitement, but mainly because of my immediate reaction. My heart sank! My image of running was lonely, pointless and painful. I enjoyed exercise with music to motivate and enough breath to socialise! Concealing my true feelings, I set out on that first asthmatic run round the block! Liz had recently had two children and presumed I was the fitter of the two, with my keep fit video and books. The brutal fact was that she was nearly scraping me off the pavement as I strove to keep up with her. I'm a quitter at heart, and when the going gets tough – I give up! As we were nearing the end of this desperate run, I was dreaming of a hot bath when Liz let the final bombshell fall. She was a marathon runner, with four under her belt, and her husband had run no fewer than 50 marathons! This silenced me as I waved her goodbye and fell into a bath, vowing never to run another step!

To cut a very long, painful story short, just twelve months later I found myself at the start of the London Marathon. If anyone had told me that this is where it would have led, I promise you that run round the block would never have occurred. Through all the cut and thrust of training, I have learnt more about my strengths and weaknesses than any teacher, psychiatrist or coach could have imparted! My failures, mistakes and pain have been punctuated by hope, discovery and tough understanding of a far greater race we are all in – the human race! This is tougher than a marathon, stretching further than 26.2 miles, with more gut-wrenching twists and turns and long uphill hauls. It exhilarates and exhausts, challenges and chokes, builds and breaks, fulfils and frustrates. We enter at birth, and are reluctantly reminded of laps at strategic birthdays. But what is it all for? What lies at the end? A medal? A cup? Joy, or just darkness, loneliness and death?

Back to a breathless beginner! In order to impress my new friend Liz, I attempted to build up my stamina on lone early morning runs. Avoiding the watchful eyes of neighbours, postmen and milkmen, I escaped to the isolation of St Catherine's Hill and Hengistbury Head, with squirrels, deer and seagulls as my companions. Isolation, the image of running that had caused me to avoid it for so long, was becoming strangely attractive. I grew accustomed to solitude and the sound of silence. This spasmodic, 'run around' nature of mine was becoming slowly aware of long-distance commitment, and the thrill of going beyond your capability and comfort zone.

Within a few months, my 'run round the block' had stretched to six miles, and I was invited by Liz and Steve to join their running club in Poole. Running alone had become my security. The thought of running an extended ten miles with others threatened me. All my fellow runners were stronger and more experienced, and the discouragement was deafening as I was slowly abandoned entering the seventh mile. I had never broken six miles, and my legs knew it! I ground to a pathetic plod, desperately trying to climb Poole's famous Gravel Hill. The evening light was fading, and without the support and guidance of the other runners I was lost. A novice to long-distance running, I hit the wall early. My head dropped forward in exhaustion. Just visible in the darkness were my trainers stumbling to a painful shuffle. My vulnerability prevented me from grinding to a halt. Suddenly, in the gloom, another pair of running shoes appeared. The twilight and weariness prevented me from seeing whom they belonged to. They were much bigger, much dirtier, and much more well-worn than mine. The incredible comfort when those trainers came into step with mine was unforgettable! I was no longer alone, and that assurance got me through the next mile. Sensing my returning discouragement, a much deeper voice than mine breathed, 'Come on, girl, we're going to get through this together!'

Approaching busy junctions, my fellow runner got between the traffic and me and protectively guided me safely through and home. On arrival, I fell exhausted into the shower, never seeing the owner of the running shoes. Questioning their presence with me later, I was advised of a powerful policy of the club. All expert runners take their turn as 'sweepers'. Their main concern being to protect and encourage, they sweep round the back of training runs, to ensure no runner is hurt, lost or abandoned. My personal sweeper had run a marathon the day before, and was willing to limp around with me on a mere ten-mile run, to get me home!

We are not alone in the human race. There is one who comes alongside, plants his feet in step with ours, urges us on, and, if necessary, picks us up! There is no circumstance in which he would abandon us. His main aim is to keep us going, and to teach us through the tough times. If my sweeper had allowed me to give up at Gravel Hill, I would never have made it to the marathon. I met him face to face, for the first time, at the end of that gruelling 26 miles 385 yards in London. Having seen only his well-worn running shoes at our first meeting, I was mystified, these several months later, at the congratulations and pride of this handsome young man for my achievement. When he saw my puzzled face, he introduced himself and said, 'I stuck by you on your first long training run – don't you remember?' The memories came flooding back. His care and commitment on that lonely run have had a lasting effect on me, and it was great to be able to thank him personally.

My personal sweeper in the human race is called *Parakletos* – a name that powerfully describes God the Holy Spirit. Not someone to be scared of but, as the name indicates, someone who comes right alongside us and who is expert in the human race! He is not a distant deity, removed from our struggles in life. He is God, who clothed himself in the human strip to run the race before us. He got stuck into the day-to-day marathon of family life and a carpentry apprenticeship with his dad. He knew loneliness, bereavement, rejection and peer pressure. His marathon did not stretch 26.2 miles, but spanned 33 long years. It was known and prepared for throughout eternity. There was no medal at the end of his marathon, just abandonment by his teammates and close friends. Wrong accusation, crowd abuse, torture led to the cruel climax – death on a Roman cross! Why on earth did he do it? It was because here on earth was the only place he could show us how much he loved us: 'For God loved the world so much that he gave his only Son, so that everyone who believes in him may not die but have eternal life' (John 3:16 GNB).

Eternal life is a life of quality as well as quantity. God, through his Son Jesus, broke through every wall we can hit in life, progressing to the one wall of certainty for us all: death! The product of our sin has finally been broken through and conquered. I am writing this chapter on Good Friday, and it would not have been possible if Jesus were still on the cross or lying in the tomb. The cross and the tomb are empty; Jesus ran through them, smashing their power over us, to give us the victorious life he always intended for us. As we invite a living God into our own personal marathon, he brings with him stamina, stickability and power.

Stretching exercises

1. I dare you to do something different! (Run, walk, cycle, swim or do armchair exercise.)
2. Share in a friend's chosen activity.
3. Who has stuck by you in your human race (in the past, present or both)? Are you still in touch with them? Send them a card to thank them, or thank them again face to face.
4. Identify some of life's marathons you have been through. (Family crisis, sickness or failure.) If it helps, write them down, and thank God for sticking with you, even when you felt he had abandoned you. Thanksgiving is a spiritual exercise that strengthens your heart and mind!

> Don't worry about anything, but in all your prayers ask God for what you need, always asking him with a thankful heart. And God's peace, which is far beyond human understanding, will keep your hearts and minds safe in union with Christ Jesus. (Philippians 4:6–7 GNB)

5. Stretch your mind by memorising Hebrews 13:5 – 'Never will I leave you; never will I foresake you.'

LAP 2

Running Strip

I have a problem. Reading through the previous chapter has caused a blip in my writing. I cannot write about something I am not doing. My inspiration comes from involvement. I reluctantly admit I must run in order to write! The basics of my school life were the 3Rs: reading, writing and arithmetic. They now have become reading, writing and running . . . and, boy, did I know it today as I burst into the neighbourhood! This was more like freezing, frightening and far from funny! It took me back to those early days when I crept out in the darkness. Not only am I a 'short, sharp burster', but I also like my creature comforts. Amazed neighbours, postmen and milkmen grew accustomed to seeing a top-heavy bundle of humanity gasping its way painfully around Christchurch. To combat the damp and cold, I would throw everything on in sight: thermals, tracksters, coats, gloves, sweaters, scarves and balaclavas! You name it; I wore it! It did not take me long to discover the handicap they became part way round the distance.

It is amazing how many experts materialise when word gets round you are attempting the London Marathon. Runners or not, they advise you what to wear and what not to wear, where to run and where not to run, what to eat and what not to eat, and I became the recipient of various training books and fitness manuals. I browsed through many, but the one that had been around the longest came to my aid on those cold, dark mornings. The first of three vital guidelines in a chapter on 'When the going gets tough' provided a practical solution. 'Throw off everything that hinders.' My extra clothing had become soaked and heavy as the run progressed. Scarves hindered my breathing, and hats caused my head to throb. Thermals plus the tracksters tightened my legs, and their heaviness hampered my progress. Weighed down, overheated and exhausted, I longed to strip them off and run free. To avoid obvious scandal, I learnt quickly to wear suitable clothing. My running strip needed to be the basic necessities for protection and support, lightweight and non-restrictive. The liberating lesson of leaving behind the unnecessary was much appreciated.

How about the human race? We can carry around the constricting clutter of childhood, the tyranny of our teens, family feuds, failure, heartache, guilt and inadequacy. When the going gets tough they stifle, choke and weigh us down. If only, as on the computer, there was a 'back space' key to obliterate all that we don't want that has gone before! The clinging strip of guilt continually wraps its insidious tentacles around us. Tangled with my pride and standards instilled in me through childhood, it was more like a straitjacket on me as I hit the wall of parenting a few years back. The constrictive clothing was now squeezing tightly, deep down into my heart. My usual 'bounce back' nature was painfully handicapped. I was reminded of words used by my maths teacher at school, in rebuke of my careless approach to figures. 'You're fit for nothing!' This was not just sums at school, but sons at home. Two young men, full of life and energy, whom I loved dearly and I felt I had failed. With problems of the heart, our emotions run haywire, and when not shared, can magnify and mangle our perspective.

What I now see as an important stage of their personal marathon, I then viewed, through my vulnerability, as rebellion and complete rejection of all that we had taught them. I had thoroughly enjoyed being both Mum and Dad to Stephen and Duncan in their childhood and early teens. I loved the challenge of running the home and family as Doug travelled up and down the country. I lapped up the praise that came in recognition of my lonely task. In a sense, I had been their coach and guide in the human race, and felt a certain amount of pride in their journey.

This was before I hit the wall of teenage independence, when I had to learn to let go. In throwing off the 'nagging mother' strip, I halted the suffocation of our relationships. But my involvement in the church and speaking throughout the country had caused me to become more concerned about the expectations of others than the needs of my sons and what God had in store for them. The simple instruction 'throw off everything that hinders' has been a process of several years that has taught me much about unconditional love, understanding and acceptance. These are all 'long-distance' commitments. Our disposable society, with its crushing, recycling and replacing mentality, doesn't expect things to last, and tends to throw off the commitment rather than work through the hindrances. I was learning slowly not to sacrifice my sons on the altar of other people's opinions, and to experience the depth and understanding that comes in our relationships when we run through the tough walls together.

Back to my training books. I am not a great studier of manuals. Talking and thinking about training causes me to lose it mentally. I'm a 'spur of the moment' sort of person. I'd rather get on and do it than talk and read about it! This all changed when I dug out my old manual. I had known it as a reference book for many other areas, but to find it helped so practically in marathon running was a revelation. I should not have been surprised. The chapter on 'When the going gets tough' is in fact a letter written to the Hebrews by Paul to combat fatigue and discouragement. He concludes his training paragraph with: '... so that you will not grow weary and lose heart' (Hebrews 12:3).

It was on returning from one of my 'top heavy' runs that these words caught my eye. I scoured the previous sentences, and recognised the relevance of this first instruction: 'Let us throw off everything that hinders.' The humour of the moment hit me, as I collapsed in a heap! I was so tired and tangled up with damp clothes that it was impossible to throw them off. Slowly, and with much moaning, I tugged and peeled myself free. The same applies to our human race. As I sank thankfully into a steaming bath, I reflected how tough it is just to throw off childhood memories of abuse, years of pain and agony, bereavement, failure, rejection and inadequacy.

This hit me with full force recently when praying with a close friend. She had struggled with guilt since childhood, carrying this horrendous load in silence, and keeping quiet every time she had longed to share it. As the words eventually spilled out of her mouth, the agony of years was dealt with. My friend was one of twins, and from childhood had believed she was responsible for the death of her twin brother at birth.

This is just one painful example of how memories from child-hood can haunt us and hinder our progress. In the marathon, sometimes discouragement and weariness caused me to gasp, 'I can't go on; this is too difficult.' I was wrong! It's not just too difficult, it's impossible without the author of my running manual. This is God himself, who laid aside his majesty, threw off his splendour, and freed himself of everything that was a hindrance to the healing of our relationship with him.

Born as a vulnerable baby to a teenage mother, he donned the human strip, identifying powerfully with our present day and age. He ran through every lap of life that we do, and so much more. That first guideline in Hebrews is not quite complete. God's training schedule starts with, 'Let us throw off everything that hinders and the sin that so easily entangles.' It is not so much the major sins I have a problem with, but the wrong attitudes, intentions and desires that cause havoc in my daily marathon. That's why God gave up everything for me and sent his Son Jesus to break through the wall of death, and to take on himself all that I need to throw off! He, who knew no sin, became sin for me. All the torture and torment since time began was hurled on him as he hung on the cross. Personal, national, and worldwide, our sin was dealt with once and for all as he cried, 'It is finished!' Having smashed through death and the grave, he waits patiently for us to do our bit. The first step of accepting all that God has done is only the start of the most incredible journey anyone can set out on. It is tough, but with your own personal trainer alongside, there is nowhere more secure!

A trip down to the local refuse tip with my garden rubbish opened my eyes to the therapeutic action of personally throwing away my own mess that mucks up my life! So much is laid on for us today that we take it for granted. On my return, I sat down to list on paper the anxieties that were crowding my mind. Reluctantly, I included the sins that had entangled my life. Recognising them, and getting them out of my system, enabled me literally to lay them before God and ask his forgiveness. I then tore them up and put the pieces in a dustbin bag, along with all the other useless rubbish. To see that bag hurtle into the skip at the refuse tip reminded me of the words in Psalm 103:12, 'As far as the east is from the west, so far does he remove our sins from us' (GNB).

Anxiety is the most inhibiting 'strip' in motherhood. Stemming from natural love and concern, it magnifies failures and disfigures our judgement. As our sons flexed their muscles of independence, I reacted out of insecurity and hurt, aggravating situations unnecessarily. I could run, but I couldn't hide from my lack of understanding of them and my loss of communication with them. It was my personal trainer who reminded me of his endless experience with wayward children! I was number one on his list!

Matthew 23:37 reflects powerfully the mother heart of God: 'How often I have longed to gather your children together, as a hen gathers her chicks under her wings, but you were not willing.' I read about the aching heart of Hagar, a mum agonising over her son, in Genesis 21:16: 'While she was sitting there, she began to cry' (GNB). I could identify with that, and eagerly read on. Hagar was at a loss to know what to do for her son, as he was dying of thirst. Water had run out, and she couldn't bear to see Ishmael slipping away. I, too, felt the desperation of family relationships dying and communication running out.

The angel told her, 'Get up, go and pick him up, and comfort him.' I am sure Hagar obeyed immediately. I was frustrated. This instruction had gone to the heart of my problem. I could no longer pick up and comfort grown men. Mummy could no longer make it better! They didn't appear to need any help or comfort; they could manage very well, thank you! This was what was dragging me down; I was redundant. After a day of arguing with God, I finally read the solution in the following verses: 'Then God opened her eyes, and she saw a well . . . God was with the boy as he grew up' (Genesis 21:19–20 GNB).

My anxiety had blinded me to the real needs of teenagers. God, who knows us all inside out, wanted to open my eyes to his opportunities for picking up and comforting grown men. Just as Hagar saw the vital ingredient to save Ishmael, so through many years I have been seeing God's creative ways of encouraging Steve and Duncan. Days of fishing, dashes to the airport for sights of unique aircraft, working together on a keep fit video, and asking and acting on their advice, especially where computers are concerned, all strengthened our flagging communication. It's now me who feels the irresponsible teenager, as our two grown sons will caution me with, 'Are you sure you should be running in the Marathon, Mum? How old are you?'

Anxiety continues to creep up on me in the human race, but I have learnt the words and exercise of 1 Peter 5:7: 'Cast all your anxiety on him because he cares for you.' We need to work out that verse regularly.

I have left the most important pieces of our running gear until last. They are crucial to long distances and caused me the most problems in the early days. My run round the block saw my feet in old plimsolls. I hobbled around for days afterwards, with bruised toes and aching arches. Feet are the foundation to running, and it is vital to have the correct size and width shoe. I have always worn a size six shoe and had no problem at all. The long distance haul adds more pressure, and literally shakes your foundations, causing havoc in the hidden areas. I have an extremely long second toe on my right foot. I kept telling myself it was very small, hidden and unimportant. The nail started to turn black, and the pain increased. Eventually, that seemingly insignificant, hidden digit rendered my whole body useless! My running ground to a halt for several weeks because of ill-fitting shoes. I have tried many different manufacturers of running shoes, but my latest pair has been the best for that tricky toe: they do the half sizes and extra width and are called 'New Balance'.

With the reopening of St Catherine's Hill here in Dorset after the foot and mouth epidemic, Doug and I decided to celebrate by christening our new shoes in the grass and mud of the countryside. After weeks of pounding the streets of Christchurch, it was great to escape from the exhaust fumes and roar of traffic, to hear the birds and smell the breath of spring. The bluebells were pushing their way through the stinging nettles, and every branch was bursting with new life. The squirrels and rabbits were scuttling away in all directions, and our new shoes were ideal for the uneven ground and sudden muddy patches. Their bright newness was fast fading to a mud bespattered brown, but what security and firmness they gave us as we hurtled downhill to return along the footpaths, through the rhododendrons and trees towards home. Picking our way through tree roots and ferns, we rounded a bend on our well-worn route, to be drawn to a sudden halt!

Blocking the way ahead was a mini lake, with a concerned lady plucking up courage to balance her way across a carefully laid log. She was beautifully dressed, with high-heeled shoes, but with a very anxious expression. With the grip and balance of our shoes, plus the speed, we could have bounced with ease across that log, but it was very evident this lady needed support. With true East End chivalry, Doug offered our help. With Doug leading her, and me steadying her from behind, we guided her safely across that slippery makeshift bridge, high heels and all! Calling our apologies for not having a cloak to lay down for her, we raced off home! In retrospect, that mini rescue could not have taken place without the support and balance of our running shoes.

How is your footwear in the human race? In an insecure world, with shifting standards and falling morals, our foundations are shaken or non-existent. You can experience a new balance in life as you kick off ill-fitting slippers and have your feet personally fitted with the readiness that comes from the gospel of peace. These can be found in Ephesians 6:15. The deep-down peace and security that comes from this good news gives us a sure-footed readiness for anything life throws at us, and enables us to introduce others to our personal guide and trainer, Jesus Christ himself.

Stretching exercises

1. Identify hindrances in your human race (e.g. low self-esteem, bad memories, failure, handicap). Explore what helps you deal with them. (Talking them through? Writing them down? Praying them through?)
2. Memorise 1 Peter 5:7: 'Cast all your anxiety on him because he cares for you.'
3. Recall some of the positive things that were said to you as

a child. Now write down one negative memory. It might have been a word or an action. Ask God to remove any destructive influence that memory has on you now. Memorise Psalm 103:12: 'As far as the east is from the west, so far does he remove our sins from us' (GNB). Now tear up or burn that piece of paper, and be reassured that God not only removes our sins that we ask forgiveness for, but also the effect of sins committed against us. Forgiving those who have wronged us is tough! Remember our fellow runner is the expert example in this area. 'Father, forgive them!' he gasped, as he hung dying from a cross, laden down with sin he did not commit. If we ask him, he will help us and release us from any bitterness.

4. How is the exercise going? From a leisurely walk to a workout in the gym, all exercise releases tension and improves our well-being.

LAP 3

Running On Empty

I lay motionless on the ground, with a small group of youngsters circled around me, not knowing what to do. Every ounce of air had been knocked out of me and the effect my empty lungs were having was frightening. I couldn't move, speak or even cry. Just seconds before, I had been enjoying my favourite pastime, climbing trees on Wandsworth Common. My little gang knew all the trees in our London playground, and had been swinging round a circle we called our Monkey Puzzle. The branches were slightly damp, and as I launched my eight-year-old body out into space to grasp the highest branch, my hands slipped and I plummeted horizontally to earth, to discover what true winding is all about! I had never experienced it before, nor have I since that memorable incident.

As lively little tree climbers, we spent most of our time avoiding and hiding from the brown uniformed common keepers. The sudden appearance of one now was to be my saving. Without a word he administered the vital first aid and restored the pattern of breathing that was necessary for me to keep going. Because I was fully conscious throughout that fall and the effects after, I remember with brutal clarity the contrast between empty and full lungs! It was like being frozen in a fraction of time. The warmth and relief that flooded my body as my lungs filled with air again has stayed firmly in my memory ever since. Needless to say, the restoring of my breathing had me running around again in no time.

The cry of a newborn baby announces life, as the lungs commence their intended function for that little body separated from his mum. From then on we take breathing so much for granted, only focusing on it when emergencies affect this vital function. On my first run round the block, my lungs were not used to this sudden activity. I was longing to stop, and was fast running out of breath. The hard facts were that there was plenty of air, but my lungs were not used to operating at such a rate. Their capacity and efficiency needed to be built up slowly. My 'immediate' temperament wanted results right away, but I was about to start out on the new experience of gradual, long-distance improvement that lasts longer than the short, sharp bursting approach!

'The Fall' is often used to describe mankind's decision to go it alone, to leave God out. As we took the plunge, sin knocked the spiritual breath out of us. In the human race, we are running on empty. Although physically alive, we need to be resuscitated spiritually. Many have described it as the aching void within, and try to fill the emptiness with work, relationships, money, or various religions and cults. Just as my heroic common keeper saw the painful dilemma I was in, and came up with the solution, so God, who had been abandoned at the beginning of time, never gave up on us. Though rejected, he went through death on a cross to rise again. He is the life he offers: life that has knocked out the finality of death. I could have refused the first aid on Wandsworth Common, and would have deserved the result. God does not force first aid on us, but offers long-distance aid – in fact, everlasting salvation – as a gift. It's ours for the taking, when we come to him accepting all he has done. As we step out in faith, God breathes spiritual life into our human marathon. Prayer can be described as our spiritual breathing. It is not a lifeless rule, but a living relationship with God himself. Step by step, mile by mile, day by day, God builds up our spiritual stamina; he increases our capacity to breathe in deeply all his ability to help us reach our full potential. This isn't a crutch to lean on. He's our Creator to learn from, our own 'spiritual Sweeper', fellow runner and coach.

'Throw off everything that hinders' (Hebrews 12:1) happens automatically in our breathing. We exhale carbon dioxide, which would poison the system, and we absorb the oxygen, which is so vital for our survival. So with our ever-growing relationship with God: he supplies all that is necessary for our spiritual growth, and helps us discard all that poisons and prevents growth. Take those early months of running as an example. I had learnt to throw off the unnecessary clothes that hindered my progress, but now I had a problem with calories! In our diet-conscious age, where unless you are a certain weight, size and shape, you really haven't made it, I desperately needed to pile the calories on. Always having enjoyed my food, I was continuing my usual three good meals a day. The difference now was the daily run which burnt off all the calories. The weight was falling off me and I was running out of steam! Liz gently advised me to up my intake, and eat plenty of carbohydrates, like pasta and potatoes. I never wanted to see another strand of spaghetti again! There were times when I was not hungry, but knew I must eat to prepare for the following day's run. It was either force-feed or fall flat! I might not enjoy the meal at the time, but what a difference it made in my run the next day. I appreciated the strength and energy it gave me, and kept going longer as a result.

Food has changed dramatically down through the years. We have gone from the 'meat and two veg' to take-aways, fast foods, microwave meals and every nation's food on our door-step! There is so much at our disposal, with the *Ready, Steady, Cook* style television programmes tickling our taste buds and urging us to sample new foods and recipes. The world is lit-erally your oyster, if you like seafood! Slowly, I experienced the difference an increased, balanced diet, plus plenty of fresh air, made to my gradually extended runs. On my return from new, longer runs, I would jump in the car and check the dis-tance on the milometer. The feeling of excitement and achievement when the indicator went further than expected did more for my mental fitness as I returned home exhausted physically. Mental fitness is equally important in preparing for a marathon as building up miles in the legs! What we feed our minds, and the different people we listen to, can spur us on or leave us standing.

My childhood and teen years involved no television. I didn't miss what I never had. Meeting and marrying Doug introduced me to the 'Box'. After a very active and full life of teaching, I was thankful for its company when the children came along. With Doug often away, and the boys asleep by seven, my media watching increased. In my loneliness and TV naivety, I watched anything and everything, from depressing news items to dubious dramas. I soaked up a diet

of violence, sex, depression and fear. The occasional good programmes were swallowed up by the bad ones. I was hooked!
As all diets affect your appearance and behaviour, I became
tired, depressed and disheartened.

In desperation, I cried out to God. I needed to throw off the
compulsive viewing that was hindering my outlook and daily
living. My nightly mental meals were crippling me, but I
found it impossible to switch off. The Holy Spirit, my personal trainer, understood my frustration and loneliness. He
coached me to pray within my weakened faith. Hesitantly, I
requested that he fill my time with other interests, and occupy
my mind with situations and needs that would crowd out the
wrong use of TV. In retrospect, I can see now what then I
longed to see overnight: God has powerfully answered that
weak cry for help. Out of my isolation, and long, lonely even-
ings, there has grown a friends and neighbours outreach, keep
fit, house groups and 'Hot Potato' discussion sessions. They
mushroomed into daytime activities, with lunch outreach,
'mums and toddlers' and 'Busy Bees' pre-school activity
mornings. More recently, Alpha and parenting groups have
occupied me morning, noon and night! The little time I have
left is filled with writing, running, and mastering a word pro-
cessor, often throughout the night. As we fix our eyes on Jesus,
and work through our hindrances with his Spirit, he reassures
us with: 'Throw off everything that hinders . . . so that you will
not grow weary and lose heart' (Hebrews 12:1, 3).

In training for the London Marathon, I was so thankful to
feed on Steve's and Liz's wisdom. They were seasoned marathon runners who had started from scratch themselves. They
didn't nag or use words like 'training' or 'discipline'! This
would have been a complete turn-off for me. Instead, they
took time to suggest new runs that might interest me. On

occasions, I cycled alongside them to see the new routes, and hear their down-to-earth comments on how they felt, and what helped them at different stages of the run. They shared their weaknesses and strengths, and I was allowed a valuable glimpse into the heart and mind of runners on the run. This fed my mind with a determination not to give up. I was learning so much now that spilled over into my human race.

We live in a visual day and age. Our minds are continually fed through the television, Internet, newspapers, films and magazines. Communication is immediate and persuasive. There is much that is helpful and strengthens our minds, but too often we are fed a diet of violence, sex, fear, destruction and death. These are the ingredients that stay in our minds and hearts, destroying our peace and slowing us down. They cause insecurity, and are so often the recipe for depression and breakdown. Switching off from the real world is not the answer, so how do we keep going when bad news is what sells papers, and we are starved of any taste of hope and happiness?

The best-selling book of all time has the answer. In Matthew we read of the biggest picnic ever! 'The number of those who ate was about five thousand men, besides women and children' (Matthew 14:21). The overall number must have easily exceeded 10,000! We learn from Mark's record of the same event that many of the crowd, in their excitement and curiosity, had run from all the towns to see Jesus. After their cross-country exercise, and hours of listening and watching Jesus in the fresh air, we can have no doubt that this was a starving multitude! The final understatement comes from one of Jesus' closest friends. John sums up in just a few simple words the incredible result of distributing just five small barley loaves and two fishes to this vast crowd: '... and they all had as much as they wanted' (John 6:11 GNB). The 'leftovers' were far more than the young boy's picnic – twelve baskets full! I have just taken a hot, fruity bread pudding out of the oven and sampled a slice. Imagine how many I could have made from the twelve baskets of breadcrumbs.

The following day, the crowds caught up with Jesus in Capernaum. Many of them were fascinated by the miracle of the day before, and sought Jesus for the spectacular – and maybe another free meal. However, others had experienced a deeper hunger from the words of Jesus and just being with him. Since he had left them, the emptiness within had grown, and their search for him was urgent. Hanging on his every word, they listened to the debate and asked their questions. One powerful answer from Jesus grabbed their attention and cut across all their questions: 'Then Jesus declared, "I am the bread of life. He who comes to me will never go hungry, and he who believes in me will never be thirsty"' (John 6:35). He couldn't be talking of the bread and water from the day before: the crowds would have already eaten meals since then, and some would no doubt have had hunger pangs after their journey to Capernaum. No! Jesus went right to the heart of the aching void that causes spiritual hunger and thirst. We were created to run in the human race with God. Without him, we are running on empty. We constantly hunger and thirst after something more than this fleeting life offers. As we welcome Jesus into our personal marathon, he brings with him the fullness of his very own Spirit, which satisfies the hunger and thirst of every area of our lives. We need to ask him regularly to fill us, feed us and refresh us. This is a prayer we can be confident he will answer if we mean business.

Stretching exercises (alone and in groups)

1. Not all television viewing is wrong. Share the programmes that help you and why.
2. Share any hindrances in viewing. How do you overcome these?
3. Inhale deeply through your nose. Exhale through your mouth. Remembering the natural process of absorbing the good (oxygen) and getting rid of the bad (carbon dioxide), try this mental and spiritual exercise. Breathe in God's peace; breathe out your fear. Breathe in God's strength; breathe out your weakness. Deep breathing calms us down, and with this added exercise can help us pray more specifically for our needs.
4. In twos, say what is your favourite meal. Provide the recipe if you cook it. Describe the ingredients if you eat out. Now describe a spiritual meal you have had from the Bible. Turn to it, and explain how it fed you.
5. Start reading one of the Gospels. Enjoy walking through it with Jesus. Imagine yourself right there with him. Listen to him, and feed your mind and heart with his living words.
6. Memorise John 6:35: 'I am the bread of life. He who comes to me will never go hungry, and he who believes in me will never be thirsty.'

LAP 4

You Can Run, But You Can't Hide

American boxer Jo Louis was training for a World Heavyweight Championship fight. Tactics were being discussed with his trainer and his coach. All three had closely studied his opponent, and knew what they were up against. Jo listened intently to the observations and advice of his mentors, until the coach stressed, 'He'll dance away from you, and run rings round you.' With the conviction of a champion, Jo replied, 'He can run, but he can't hide!'

In my early, vulnerable months of running, I was playing 'hide-and-seek'. Hiding in the darkness, escaping to the countryside, and searching for answers. I found I could think more clearly when I was running, and unscramble my confused mind. My 'run around' nature needed action to sort through the many changes that had occurred in recent months. It was clear that my lifestyle had to change. Our parents were ageing and needing more care and possible future nursing. With both Doug and myself travelling constantly, time with family urgently needed to be reviewed. There was an unrest stirring within me about our future and where we were going. Call it a mid-life crisis if you like, but, as in the Marathon, this wall seemed impenetrable!

The implications of this crisis caused me at times to run away from Doug, God and myself. 'Running around like a headless chicken' was a good description of me at that time! I stopped reading the Bible for fear of what God might say to me. I enjoyed my travelling and the variety of situations and venues I was invited to speak in: sports centres, prisons, youth clubs, schools, hotels, pubs, coffee bars, clubs, universities and churches. Life wasn't boring, and I was reluctant to change. I could run, but I couldn't hide. Powerful, old-fashioned words, memorised from the Authorised Version of the Bible as a child, crept up on me unawares. I found myself echoing them: 'Whither shall I go from thy spirit? or whither shall I flee from thy presence?' (Psalm 139:7av). These words were very descriptive of my escape into the hills! They were also a timely reminder of my faithful 'Sweeper' who, however fast I fled or deviously I dodged, always kept in touch with me. Later, as I reminded myself of David's words in Psalm 139, God reassured me of his commitment to me: '. . . even there your hand will guide me, your right hand will hold me fast'(Psalm 139:10).

Tough decisions had to be made, and I desperately needed the expert in my marathon close at hand, with advice for the way ahead. In my impatience, I longed to see through the next few years as they stretched out before me. God was teaching me very practically through my running that to see too far ahead is not good for us.

Training was slowly progressing. My longer runs had now stretched to 15 miles once a week, with shorter ones for speed, and gentle, recovery jogs for smelling the roses! I was allowed one precious day off. At first, I enjoyed a new, picturesque route for the longer run. After growing up in London, with the city life and buildings shutting out the skyline, it was amazing to run free down by the seashore. My eyes could see for miles in all directions. The different moods of the sea fascinated me as it stretched tirelessly out towards the horizon. Never had I seen so much sky, with clouds of all shapes and sizes racing me to the end of the promenade. Bournemouth Pier is a favourite landmark for many holidaymakers as they travel south for a well-earned break. Strangely, it became an eyesore to me in those months preceding the marathon. After running six miles round and over Hengistbury Head, I caught that rare sight of a four-mile uninterrupted stretch of sea front, running away from home. The wind annoyingly seemed to hit me full blast in the face as I surfaced the Head and ran down towards the sea. A rare beauty spot in the summer became a rough, brutal stage of my training! I struggled with the constant visual reminder of the distance I still had to cover, before turning away from the pier and the sea to return home. The temptation was always there to cut the run short and leave that open, tough haul behind. I was grasping at what lay too far ahead, and losing sight of the close, achievable goals: Boscombe Pier came before Bournemouth, and friends' beach huts came before the famous zigzag paths up the cliffs. Dog walkers and skateboarders were greeted and negotiated! Strategically placed water taps were spotted and used regularly, until suddenly Bournemouth Pier loomed large and attainable, as it was passed and left behind. In retrospect, I was escaping from the present in my human race, hiding from the here and now, as I raked the horizon ahead for hope.

'Your right hand will hold me fast' (Psalm 139:10) is a

reminder of God the Holy Spirit's helping hand in preventing us seeing too far ahead. He knows every step of the journey and will prepare us for it by guiding us through the immediate landmarks in our human race. My number one priority, and immediate goal, was those closest to me. My ever-accelerating occupation was literally driving me away from them all. Doug and I passed each other on the motorway on occasions, going in the opposite direction. Steve and Duncan spoke to us on the phone at times when we should have been together. Our parents were neglected as they were growing older, and last, but by no means least, my personal Sweeper was being swept aside. God, my number one guide and instructor, was being ignored. As I faced up to this immediate challenge, instead of searching for the uncertainty beyond, it became crystal clear that I should return home. This was not quitting and cutting the run short; it was, in fact, adjusting to the expert's route, which opened up the years ahead in an entirely new way. I emerged from hiding to continue my run on course.

Hill running was a complete contrast to the long, flat stretch of seaside. I could never see further than the brow of the hill, the top of a tree, or the light at the end of a tunnel of under-growth. The sudden breathtaking views from the steep inclines would then vanish, as I plunged down into a gully of gorse, negotiating sudden twists and turns and accumulated water and mud in the crevices. It was partly my adventurous spirit in the early months of running that caused me to avoid the main footpaths over the hills. I loved the challenge of breaking new ground, but I was still not coping with onlook-ers. I would rather retreat into a tunnel of tangled under-growth, protruding tree roots and stinging nettles than face the laughing comments from passers-by. I tripped over the roots, fell headlong into tearing brambles, but still preferred my tunnel of pain to facing up to the real world. My inward-looking perspective had lost sight of the panoramic view at the top of the hill!

The mighty marathon runner we read of in 1 Kings 18:46 is Elijah the prophet. His mountaintop experience is on Mount Carmel, up against 450 prophets of Baal and 400 prophets of Asherah with King Ahab himself. He is outnumbered, and the odds are very much against him. His challenge is not to a marathon but to a 'prayerathon'. They are to call on the name of their god Baal to send down fire to consume the sacrifice of a bull. Elijah will call on the name of the Lord, whom Israel has abandoned: 'The god who answers by fire – he is God' (1 Kings 18:24). Elijah allows them a head start, and they set off in the morning.

Their gentle pleading grows to frantic shouting by noon, and following Elijah's jeering it grows to a crescendo of crazy dancing and slashing themselves with knives. Blood is flowing, but no fire is burning! By evening, we are told in verse 29, 'there was no response, no-one answered, no-one paid attention'.

Elijah quietly repairs the altar of the Lord that has been neglected. He arranges the wood in place, and the sacrificial bull on top. He asks for four large jars of water to saturate the offering. This is done no fewer than three times, until the whole altar is running with water. His first powerful prayer is closed with a plea for his nation in verse 37: 'Answer me, O Lord, answer me, so these people will know that you, O Lord, are God, and that you are turning their hearts back again.'

The fire falls immediately and devours everything in sight, consuming the sacrifice, wood, stones, soil and water! The people fall prostrate in acknowledgement of the one true God.

After severe drought and famine, foretold by Elijah, he now reassures Ahab that torrential rain is on its way. As the storm clouds gather, Ahab hitches up his chariot and races off to Jezreel, to beat the storm: 'The power of the Lord came upon Elijah and, tucking his cloak into his belt, he ran ahead of Ahab all the way to Jezreel' (1 Kings 18:46).

This was a run of incredible speed and distance. Outrunning a chariot over a distance of 17 miles cross-country, after a day of immense pressure, is amazing. What victory Elijah has experienced! Yet within hours he has given up and is running for his life! He escapes 100 miles to Beersheba, to avoid the lethal threats of a woman, Jezebel, Ahab's wife.

There is much in the human race to cause us to run and hide, to withdraw into our tunnels of pain, and to avoid confrontation. Fear is the greatest factor in Elijah's flight. He is hated and being hunted. His natural instinct is to 'leg it'! Who of us wouldn't do the same? Bullying, discrimination, mental and physical abuse, biting criticism and family feuds just touch the top of the iceberg of fear that drives us away. Exhaustion, discouragement and depression bring Elijah's final collapse as he groans: 'I have had enough, Lord . . . Take my life' (1 Kings 19:4).

God, his divine Sweeper, is strangely silent. He realises Elijah desperately needs rest and refreshment, not sermons and lectures. He allows him to sleep and eat in preparation for the next stage of the journey. Forty days and forty nights later, Elijah arrives at Mount Horeb, where God has a special appointment with him.

'What are you doing here, Elijah?' God speaks right into the cave where he is hiding. The searching question goes right to the heart of Elijah's predicament. God knew only too well why he was there, but he wanted him to face up to his situation in order to find a solution. The prophet's answer reflects how all of us feel at some time when the going gets tough. God asks the question twice, and Elijah's two honest answers are identical. He is feeling desperately sorry for himself. After all he has done for God, he feels abandoned, alone and under threat of death. Why has all this happened to him? His down-to-earth honesty about the way he feels paves the way for God's practical direction to get Elijah out of his 'hidey-hole' and back on track.

The Lord said to him, 'Go back the way you came' (1 Kings 19:15). God still had work for him to do. He had not abandoned him, and was going to provide a soul mate for him, a fellow worker and team colleague whom he could train to follow in his footsteps. What could have been a wasted journey of ducking and diving was transformed by a direct encounter with God.

Stretching exercises

1. What helps you in times of crisis (e.g. a particular leisure activity that helps you unwind)?
2. What hinders you at these times (e.g. drinking, eating, withdrawing)? What helps one person might hinder another. Listen to and learn from one another.
3. Take a walk, run or cycle round your neighbourhood. Whether in the town or the country, what did you enjoy most about the route, and what were the frustrations?

4. Thinking back through your life, identify some of the difficult paths you have trod, and what helped you through them.

5. Are there any references from the Bible, or words of advice from other people, that have helped you? For example: 'Trust in the Lord with all your heart and lean not on your own understanding; in all your ways acknowledge him, and he will make your paths straight' (Proverbs 3:5–6). Another example is: 'The Lord helps those who help themselves!' My nan, who was widowed in the war and left with four young children, was often heard to say this with real conviction. She had learnt the hard way not to sit round and wait for it all to happen. With tremendous faith in God, who had seen her through painful times, she worked alongside him, and helped many others as a result.

6. Memorise Proverbs 3:5–6 and when you next ask the honest question, 'Why is this happening to me?' quote those words to guard your mind and heart.

7. Following the example of Elijah in 1 Kings 18:37, pray for your nation, including yourself, that hearts will be turned back to God.

LAP 5

Running Free

The year is 1942. The city is war-torn London. A young mum is struggling with two youngsters of four and five years, and a new baby. The memory of losing a father in the First World War, when she was only nine years old, flashes across her mind, as the air raid warning sounds loudly through the shopping area where she is buying her rations for the week ahead. People scuttle in all directions, disappearing through doors and down into public shelters. Edith runs in the opposite direction to all this panic. She leaves the shops behind, and races towards the open common. At first, the two lively girls enjoy the run with Mum, but this sudden race for home quickly tires them, and they are swung up into the large pram. Hanging on for dear life, they giggle their way through the trees and bushes, and cheer as they hit the top of their road on the other side of the common.

'Nearly there,' gasps Mum, as she hurtles down a deserted road, and bursts through the back door of their home. The flight does not finish until they all scramble through the stone-floored scullery, into the kitchen with its black-leaded boiler, and down the steep wooden steps into the coal cellar. With her new baby clasped to her breast, feeding hungrily, Edith sinks thankfully on to a makeshift bed with the girls curled up around her. Secure in this solid underground fortress, they tuck into a feast of Marmite sandwiches and home-made cakes. As she surveys her little ones, she breathes a sigh of relief. They are thoroughly enjoying their picnic, completely unaware of the danger overhead.

The reason for her flight home was to protect her children from public panic, and the smell of fear that pervaded the shelters and streets of London as the sirens screamed their warnings. She had an incredible gift for transforming adversity into adventure, fear into fun and panic into picnics! I have no memory at all of those fearful days, as I was that tiny baby clasped securely in the arms of her mum in that dust-filled cellar. My dad had been posted abroad, shortly after my birth, to fight for his country in the army.

The relief to emerge from that dark cellar into the sunshine, after the 'all clear' sounded, was only a faint reflection of the pure joy experienced by the whole country as it surfaced to freedom after the Second World War. My earliest memories are of growing up in a land of hope and thankfulness. Recalling the excitement of tasting a banana for the first time, and fighting over the thin slices of a Mars bar that had to be shared with the whole family, reminds me of the tight rationing that we had grown accustomed to. We started to appreciate a more varied diet, and indulged in the simple novelty of switching a light on without the curtains drawn. All our 'blackouts' had been burnt on a massive street bonfire outside our house on VE day. The worn down kerb stayed for many years after, as a constant reminder of that victorious day of freedom. The Battle of Britain was long gone, and we could run free through our childhood.

Reminiscing is said to be a therapeutic exercise. Retracing our footsteps through early years, with our 'divine Sweeper', helps us come to terms with situations and experiences that have shaped our attitudes and moulded our reactions. We need to learn from the past, yet we are not to live in the past. Unless we move on from past landmarks in our human race, good and bad, they imprison us. This will handicap us in the present and blind us to the future.

This 'blast from the past' raised a curiosity concerning my 'tunnel of pain', a favourite route over the hill in my early days of running. Retracing my steps over St Catherine's Hill, I made for the far side, overlooking the Avon Valley, a vast stretch of wet, sandy heathland. The tunnel I withdrew into was along the edge of the rising hill, until suddenly you broke free from trees, bushes and undergrowth, to be faced with the breathtaking view of the valley below. As I approached the entrance to my former concealed pathway, I started to lose all sense of direction. Trees and bushes that had once marked the well-worn route had disappeared; undergrowth had been cleared, and the sunlight and rain had transformed my 'tunnel of pain' into a safe and bright route to the top. Obstacles that had tripped me, and brambles that had torn me, had been removed. Now I could run free of hindrance to the summit. While I had rested from running, the conservation of the countryside had continued. Viewing the transformed, clear route ahead, it hit me how inhibiting the past years of negative undergrowth can be. It accumulates and blocks progress. It stifles and chokes positive growth.

God wants to conserve us. His plan is to protect us from

harm, decay and loss. The negative debris from the past hurts us in the present, and hinders our future progress. If I had stayed in the confines of that 'tunnel of pain', I would have missed out on that glorious view ahead, not to mention one of many unexpected encounters in the countryside, namely six deer in full flight cutting across my path!

> Do not cling to events of the past or dwell on what happened long ago. Watch for the new thing I am going to do! It is happening already – you can see it now! I will make a road through the wilderness and give you streams of water there . . .

Our fitness manual hits the nail on the head again in Isaiah 43:18–19 GNB. God understands we cannot forget the past. It is the way we remember it that concerns him. It's the clinging and dwelling that is so destructive. He longs to release us from the bitterness, regret and self-pity of bad memories, and the pride and complacency of good memories.

We have some powerful prayer warriors in our church family. For Eileen, it is the course through which she has run that has made her even more effective. The past few years have been particularly painful, and the temptation to cling to the loss of her husband, and how things might have been, could have stifled her prayer life and handicapped her exercising of her spiritual gift of intercession. Instead, through letting go, she has become more sensitive and effective in her gifting. These words helped her through the wall of self-pity:

> I need and I choose to hold tight to your will for me as my life moves beyond this loss. I need and choose your healing grace and mercy for my emotions. I bind myself to the truth that you will comfort and heal me, that you have plans and purposes for me

beyond this time, and they are for good. I will not insist upon a question mark where you have placed a full stop.

I have learnt from Eileen that it takes an ongoing act of the will to come through the wall of grief with Jesus.

Paul writes on the subject of 'running towards the goal' in his letter to the Philippians:

> The one thing I do, however, is to forget what is behind me and do my best to reach what is ahead. So I run straight towards the goal in order to win the prize, which is God's call through Christ Jesus to the life above. (Philippians 3:13–14 GNB)

Paul had a lot to forget! He had imprisoned and beheaded Christians, hunted them down and persecuted them. After an incredible encounter with the risen Lord on the road to Damascus, he was now travelling throughout the land preaching the good news of Jesus. As he returned to the churches where previously he caused fear and devastation, guess who was sitting in the pews? The widows! The orphans! And we think *we* have difficulty in forgetting! If Paul had not learnt the secret of dealing with his past, he could never have run free towards God's goal and fulfilled his destiny. We need to let go what God has forgiven. Our forgiveness is based on what God says, not on how we feel. Just six short verses after God urges us to let go of our past in Isaiah 43:18–19, he reassures us with these words: 'I . . . am he who blots out your transgressions . . . and remembers your sins no more' (Isaiah 43:25).

If we have been hurt by what God has allowed into our human race, we can either hang on to it or get over it. When we dwell on it and cling to it, the enemy not only takes our past, but he also gets our future. He is fighting a losing battle;

he is running scared. It is not fashionable to forgive in this day and age. Suing, retaliation and hatred cripple our society. When we step out of fashion to forgive, it sets us free and removes a powerful weapon from the devil's hand.

Stretching exercises

1. Stretch your mind with a reminiscing exercise: share a past event in your 'human race' that taught you lessons that are still helping you today. For example, failing part of my finals, when training as a teacher, taught me determination to overcome failure. I also appreciated success when it finally came!

2. Is there an occasion from the past that still hurts now? If you find it hard to share, writing it down can help you understand it. This exercise was a breakthrough for me in releasing the hurt and failure I experienced in the parenting of my youngest son through his teens. Our communication was non-existent. Writing it down channelled my frustration and clarified my feelings and thoughts. When the immediate crisis was over, I was able to share what I had written with Duncan, and we were both helped through it.

3. What helps you let go of the past? What makes you cling to the past? There is a wealth of wisdom to be found in the stories of those who have passed through tough times and have learnt to remember without clinging and dwelling. Pam shared, after a keep fit session, how the music accom-

panying our exercises helped her through her sudden bereavement. She also shared how hard it was to return to the places which were her husband's favourite haunts before he had died. For her, it was important to revisit these places, to accept her singleness, in order to continue the process of grieving. Bereavement is a very personal experience. If we, like Paul, are to move on into what God has planned for us, we must find practical ways through the hurt of the past.

4. Is there a particular place or situation you find hard to face? Do you have any advice for others?

5. Memorise Isaiah 43:18–19. Share how we can watch for the new things that God is doing – in our personal lives, in the church, the country and the world.

LAP 6

Running Blind

It was early. The roads were empty. The hill was deserted, strangely quiet and still. As I climbed higher, it seemed to be getting darker instead of lighter, but the sky was hidden from my view by the trees. I longed to reach the top and feast my eyes on the wide expanse of heathland that stretches as far as the eye can see. Leaving the last tree behind, I was met by a wall of thick mist! The higher I had run, the thicker the mist had gathered, and now the darkness was growing. As I surfaced the brow of the hill, I could see no further than a few steps in front of me! If I hadn't known the route over the hill like the back of my hand, I would have quickly become hopelessly lost!

Our personal marathons have many unexpected twists and turns, and tunnels of pain. The most bewildering times are when we cannot see the way ahead and feel lost and abandoned. Without warning, the clinging mist of depression can creep up on us and knock us for six. Unlike the victorious batsman, we don't rise to the applause, but fall beaten and bruised to the ground, often to be picked up like the ball and hit from all directions again! Sickness, bereavement, divorce, unemployment, failure, fear and hidden heartaches can cloud our horizons. We become disorientated. We're running blind.

There is an ever-increasing number of partially sighted and blind athletes running in marathons all over the world. I was challenged by the interview on Tower Bridge of a blind runner halfway through the London Marathon this year. First of all, she had enough breath to answer the questions put to her, and second, her excitement and motivation were there for all to see! She is one of the reasons I am applying to enter the next London Marathon! As I reflected on that brief encounter on television, I was reminded of a silent bystander, hovering in the background. She was not being interviewed, but without her this incredible athlete could not have achieved her dream. She was her sighted guide. Not all runners with serious sight problems need such personal support. Those who are completely blind, however, spend much time training with a sighted person.

'I get a real buzz that, despite not being able to see, and having to rely on someone else to get me around, I can run on a level with thousands of other runners.' These were the words of 58-year-old John Turnball, when he ran for the Royal National Institute for the Blind, guided by his sighted son, Chris. What an incredible father and son achievement!

There is so much to learn from those without sight! The trust and teamwork that is vital for this marathon has to be worked at over regular training sessions. Techniques have to be tried and tested. Some runners prefer to hold the elbow of their sighted guide, who runs slightly in front of them. Others hold a strap attached to the hand or elbow of the guide. A good technique for crowded streets, or off-road running on broken ground, is a tape attached round the waist or chest of the guide, which is to be held from behind by the sightless runner. They then only need a single-width path. Whatever the technique, the key is always to be in touch with their guide. Equally, they have to be in step with their guide. They search for a runner of equal fitness, working together to cover the distance. Finally, they must be in harmony with their guide, responding to their warnings, directions and encouragements.

When the way ahead is darkening in our human race, and our minds and hearts cry out for direction, the words from our 'fitness manual' bring hope. Isaiah 26:3 in the Authorised Version says: 'Thou wilt keep him in perfect peace, whose mind is stayed on thee.' The literal staying power of those words in the Hebrew gives the picture of a small boat in a violent storm. Everything loose is secured tightly to the boat. In the blinding storms of life, we must secure ourselves to God, our guide and instructor, and we will discover the peace and security of following in his steps. We will be bound together not by a visible strap or tape, as the runner and his guide, but by unswerving faith and trust in a guide who has run the race before us. He knows the route better than the back of his hand! Our names are written on the palm of his hand: that's how committed he is to us completing the race. Wherever we are in our human marathon, however thick the mist is into the future, if we have invited God our Creator to be our guide, we are promised he will not only keep in touch with us, but his hand will guide us and his right hand will hold us fast (Psalm 139:10). I proved this verse in tough reality.

Ruth and I had travelled, prayed and holidayed together for many years with our husbands. John and Ruth were well known in the area for their popular fruit and vegetable shop. They cared personally for their customers, and many travelled miles to buy their groceries from them. Their decision not to open on Sundays was respected, as their faith was backed up by their care and commitment. Early shoppers, however, were shocked one Thursday morning to find their local store firmly closed. The door, normally wide open to welcome a steady flow of customers, was locked and the blind was firmly down. Without warning, John had collapsed, and Ruth was plunged into a choking fog of pain, anxiety and panic.

Six miles across Christchurch, I was delivering my car for its MOT, completely unaware of the crisis that had hit my friend and prayer partner. With a rare free day stretching ahead of me, I planned to walk home, exploring the roads and open countryside that I normally shot past in my car. Doug was away, and the boys were at school. My time was my own and I intended to enjoy it.

An hour later found me wandering down Christchurch High Street, approaching the historic priory, still oblivious to the now life-threatening developments just two miles across the River Stour. The May morning was warming up, and the rush-hour traffic was increasing as I crossed Tuckton Bridge. Wishing to escape from the noise of the road, I cut back along the other side of the river, towards Hengistbury Head. Leaving Wick Village behind I wandered through a labyrinth of 'bungalow-lined' avenues, their gardens a multitude of flowers. A distant siren penetrated my private world. Raising my eyes from the flowers and the shrubs, I caught sight of an ambulance racing across the top of the road. I was now just 200 yards from Ruth's shop, and still in a complete mist of ignorance, aiming to return home. Running, for no reason other than a strange compulsion, I chased the ambulance. It screeched to a halt outside Ruth's and John's shop.

I shall never fully understand the mist of bereavement, shock and grieving that Ruth had to struggle through following that day when John was so suddenly taken from her. God the Holy Spirit directed me to be alongside her in those first hours and days of bereavement. His perfect guidance and timing when I was blind to the situation stands as a powerful reminder of the truth of the verse that has helped Ruth through some of the darker times: 'Trust in the Lord with all your heart and lean not on your own understanding; in all your ways acknowledge him, and he will make your paths straight' (Proverbs 3:5–6). There is teamwork here. We must acknowledge God the Holy Spirit in asking for his guidance. The Hebrew word for acknowledge is 'Yada', translated 'to know, recognise, and have awesome respect for'. These could be terms describing the personal bonding between a blind athlete and his sighted guide. The same is true of our relationship with the Holy Spirit. He needs our wholehearted trust and co-operation in adjusting our run to follow in his steps. Not just in the days of crisis, but also transforming our 'run-of-the-mill' days.

So, from keeping in touch, how do we keep in step? After four months of running alone, Doug, my husband, decided to join me. I had become very protective of my isolation. Adjusting to his long-distance mentality challenged my short, sharp bursts of speed. My mind would wander, causing my running to slow to a meditative meander (or what Doug would call 'a pathetic plod'!). His regular footsteps alongside mine challenged me to concentrate and keep going. I used to whinge and moan, but slowly I improved.

Peter, one of Jesus' closest friends and trainees, speaks from his own experience and mistakes when he challenges us in his first letter to other runners in the faith: 'To this you were called . . . that you should follow in his steps' (1 Peter 2:21). This is the rough, tough fisherman who knew what it was to abandon his guide when the way ahead became dark! He ran in the opposite direction, and denied vehemently that he ever knew Jesus. Three times he swore blind he had never followed the Nazarene. He had firsthand knowledge of the consequences of losing touch with his guide and getting out of step with him. As he watched the man he had followed for the previous three years being cruelly nailed to a Roman cross, imagine the state of his mind and heart. The darkness ahead had intensified, and the guide who had given his life direction and hope had been snatched from him. The next three days must have been particularly distressing for Peter as he groped his way through the mist of shock, grief and regret. From the depths, Peter learned that this guide would never abandon him. After rising from the dead and appearing to the disciples on a number of occasions, Jesus had a special one-to-one with Peter. Just as Peter denied him three times, Jesus gave him the opportunity to re-affirm his love for him three times. He repeated his question: 'Do you truly love me?' Peter's answer came clear and loud each time: 'Yes, Lord, you know that I love you.' The Lord's reply reinstated Peter to follow in his steps. He was to take on the shepherding of the flock, as every leader and teacher of the church family does. Peter had learnt the hard way to listen and respond to the directions of his divine guide. Jesus knew the way ahead, and would lead him safely through.

So, how do we, who cannot physically see or hear Jesus like Peter did, follow in his steps? This would be completely impossible if Jesus had not left his Spirit with us when he returned to his Father. Jesus tried to prepare his disciples for this new visitor. 'But when he, the Spirit of truth, comes, he will guide you into all truth' (John 16:13). He will run ahead of us through the mist, clearing it step by step. As we open up God's word, he will help us hear and understand God's direction. It will shed light on the way ahead.

'Your word is a lamp to my feet and a light for my path' (Psalm 119:105). We don't have to run blindly through our human race; God's Holy Spirit is there to guide us!

Stretching exercises

1. Write down verses from Scripture that have shed light on your own personal marathon, such as Proverbs 3:5–6: 'Trust in the Lord with all your heart and lean not on your own understanding; in all your ways acknowledge him, and he will make your paths straight.'
2. If you are exercising with others, share your verses. This gives the opportunity for God to speak again through you and Scripture.
3. Get into pairs, with one person blindfolded, and the other acting as their guide. Try leading by the hand, and guiding with the voice. Discuss how God has guided you.
4. What are some of the circumstances that have caused you to lose sight of the way ahead? Share them and, if possible, what helped you through them. If you find this difficult, or you are doing these exercises on your own, try writing them down, and ask God the Holy Spirit to shed light on the way ahead.
5. Revise Proverbs 3:5–6 from Lap 4. Now add Psalm 119:105: 'Your word is a lamp to my feet and a light for my path.' Memorising is an effective exercise for the mind and heart. I have a memory like a sieve! I am learning not to excuse it, but to exercise it! It really works, especially when oiled by the word of God!

LAP 7
Team Running

I was desperate to keep my position just behind the front runner. Steve, Chairman of Poole Running Club, had a personal best time of 2 hours 32 minutes 22 seconds, achieved on one of his 50 marathons. There was I, a novice to running, and just on the shoulder of such an athlete! The fact that I was on a bike and still straining to keep in touch shows the speed and gifting of this lead runner. I was still in awe of our friends Steve and Liz, even though I now ran regularly. Their commitment and dedication drove me on, and their encouragement was limitless.

The running club had organised a six-mile race through the streets of Poole, and the park, and I was one of the entrants. Steve was introducing me to the course, and as the miles slipped by my inadequacy increased with my peddling! If I was struggling to keep up with this man when cycling, how on earth could I cope on foot? As we collapsed into the car at the end of the run, Steve sensed my despondency. On our return journey, he started to reminisce about his early days of running and his first attempt at the course we had just covered. I was amazed to discover that he had been the last over the finishing line, with an ambulance following in case he collapsed.

He continued to share his more recent experiences in training. 'There can be nothing more demoralising than playing "catch up",' he said, identifying with me in my recent run. Ian Barnes, his friend and fellow runner, is a faster runner, than Steve, and he would constantly strain to keep in touch with him. 'You go on, Ian – I'm holding you up,' he would cry in desperation. 'No, I'm fine! This is a comfortable pace – no problem!' After a few more steps, he would plead again, '*Please* go on, Ian!' The reply was always the same: 'No, we'll stick together, Steve – this pace is fine.' Steve sighed as he remembered this exchange that reflected his agony of trying to keep up. He admitted that he always thought to himself: 'Yes, the pace is fine for you – but it's killing me!' His willingness to share his weakness not only encouraged me to keep going, but also emphasised his present strength, learnt through his past inadequacy.

Team running is about encouraging and developing, not exhausting and destroying. Jesus was into team running. The early church was launched with team leadership, and the members he selected were varied and full of character.

When the bell resounded round my junior school to announce break or lunch time, I was the first to erupt out of the classroom into the playground. In no time at all, we were picking teams for our favourite game. Two of the most popular children would take it in turns to choose the members of their team. Trying to look unconcerned, I would stand with a group waiting to be chosen. As the motley group of youngsters diminished, my eyes would search the faces of the selectors, urging them to choose me. The final humiliation was when there were only two of us left, the other one was chosen, and there followed an argument over who was to 'put up' with me!

Rejection is something that can eat away our self-confidence and disfigure our whole outlook on life. As we advance in years, we hide our disappointments and cover up our longing to be included. Whether it's a partner, the job or career, the team or committee, or promotion in work, we want to be specially chosen. We all long to belong, need to be needed and love to be loved. God, our divine selector, has opened up the way, through his Son's death on the cross, for us to be part of his team. However weak or inadequate we might feel, God assures us in 1 Corinthians 1:27: 'But God chose the foolish things of the world to shame the wise; God chose the weak things of the world to shame the strong.' This doesn't mean we continue to wallow in our weaknesses, but given over to God we are promised: 'My grace is sufficient for you, for my power is made perfect in weakness' (2 Corinthians 12:9). God handpicks us. His team is incomplete without us.

While here on earth, the team, picked by Jesus, was incomplete without Thomas. This vital link was weakening by the minute. Thomas was struggling to keep up with the rest of the guys and feeling left out and very alone. For some reason, known only to himself, he had not been with the other disciples when Jesus had appeared to them after his death. Their excitement in relating the spectacular news only heightened his disappointment and doubt: 'Unless I see the nail marks in his hands and put my finger where the nails were, and put my hand into his side, I will not believe it' (John 20:25).

Jesus did not abandon Thomas, or charge on ahead to emphasise his victory. No . . . He swept round the back of his team to where Thomas was struggling, and appeared again to his disciples a week later. In an understanding one-to-one with him, he gave him the opportunity to do the very thing that would banish his doubts: 'Put your finger here; see my hands. Reach out your hand and put it into my side. Stop doubting and believe' (John 20:27). Then came encouraging words for all of us who find ourselves at the 'back of the pack', with our questions and doubts: 'Because you have seen me, you have believed; blessed are those who have not seen and yet have believed' (John 20:29).

My favourite team sport at school was netball. The excitement to be chosen for the school's under-14 team is one of my clearest memories. Our sports teacher, Miss Morgan, became our trainer and coach, and we hung onto her every word. The climax of every season was the Surrey Schools Netball Tournament. It was every school's dream to win this event, and because our school had never achieved this goal, our squad was even more determined. We arrived at school early each morning to go on training runs and work at passing patterns and techniques. Miss Morgan nurtured in us a respect for one another's skills and strengths, and stressed the importance of working together. As a team of seven, we all needed each other. I needed the shooters because, as centre, I wasn't allowed in the circle, and couldn't shoot to save my life! The shooters needed me to get the ball to them in order to score.

The day of the tournament dawned bright, and we all converged on the host school. There were more than 25 schools represented, and we were the 'under dogs'. No one knew our standard of play – and we weren't sure, either! Imagine our excitement, when, several hours later, 'these unknowns' had reached the final. I can remember standing in terror at the start of that final match. Our opponents were the holders of the trophy, and seemed double my size. All the schools and supporters had stayed to see the possible upset of the year. The atmosphere was electrifying. In my 13-year-old mind, I realised how much I needed my team around me at that first centre pass. My secret sign had been given, to show the direction of the first pass, the whistle blew, and we were off. The scores see-sawed agonisingly between the teams, but when the final whistle blew we, the under-dogs, were just one goal ahead!

This was a victory I have never forgotten. It introduced me to a love of running with a team. Whether in sport, school, work, community, family or church, we benefit from the input of others. Our different strengths, skills and gifts, welded together, are far more effective than 'going it alone'.

Monday mornings are far from depressing and boring. Our church building is packed to overflowing with a cross-section of ages and generations: dads, mums, child-minders, grand-parents and children. With a team reflecting the ages and needs of this 'hive of activity', we have explored the area of an alternative programme alongside our popular Mums and Toddlers mornings. The blending together of the three generations is a powerful team, and continues to develop our 'Busy Bee' mornings. Young parents are released into their up-to-date gifting and experience, while more mature parents and grandparents can be spare pairs of hands and wise back-up. The important concept of Sunday school is developing into weekday sessions of all-age keep fit, Bible stories, craft sessions, singing and percussion playing. The sessions last for two hours, with refreshment at the end and no anxiety about disturbing Sunday services. Parents from the community are all part of the wider team as they contribute their skills in crafts. A policeman, a postman, a nurse, a doctor, a chef and a lifeguard all dressed up in their uniforms for a special Busy Bee family service presentation. The community and the church were united in a powerful way through parents and children.

Small teams are equally as important as large teams. My involvement with a team of four in recent years has had a lasting effect on me. The other three members were much younger than I, and were brand-new Christians. What a breath of fresh air they were to my spiritual fitness.

Jesus worked and prayed with his team of twelve, and within that team were a smaller group, Peter, James and John, whom he related more closely with. John was his closest friend and confidant. It is important in team running and leadership that we spend time in building strong, secure relationships. Prayer partners, triplets and groups secure the running of any activity within the church and community.

Stretching exercises

1. Share an incident from school days that caused you to feel left out or rejected. Now recall a positive memory of being included in something, which made you feel special.
2. Describe some of the team efforts you have been involved in. Include work, church and recreation. Highlight what made them a success or a failure. I learn from my mistakes, as well as my successes.
3. Memorise 1 Peter 2:9: 'But you are a chosen people, a royal priesthood, a holy nation, a people belonging to God . . .' Remind yourself of this when you next feel inadequate or left out. Pray in twos, thanking God for your prayer partner's gifts and strengths. Be specific.

START

LAP 8

Up and Running

I was down and out – literally slumped on the mat at our front door, with the pile of mail scattered in front of me. A severe strain of flu had left me weak, depressed and definitely not up and running! In my hand, I held the sheet of paper that was the final straw! I had been accepted for the London Marathon, to be held in four months' time. Thousands apply. Thousands also get turned down, and I wanted to be one of them! I only applied to satisfy Steve and Liz, and to stop any more discussion. I had felt pretty sure I wouldn't be accepted.

I have to admit, on my better runs I would dream of running with the thousands, with television cameras zooming in, and the crowds cheering! However, the reality of the long haul always brought me down to earth. On this dark December day, the very last thing I wanted to do was run a marathon! Before the illness had hit me, I had been coping quite well with the short, faster runs, and the weekly longer stretch covering the sea front, or over the hills. I had been gently introduced to hill exercises that built up the stamina, varying paced runs, and one that was my favourite, called the 'recovery', which allowed me to rest, walk or jog as required. What a vast contrast now, as I could hardly crawl into the kitchen to make a cup of tea!

Long-distance running needs mental fitness, as well as physical fitness. My mind and body were in agreement this time as I viewed the next 16 weeks. My quitting nature reared its pathetic head as I took the last of my antibiotics. Not only had my body taken a beating from the bug, but, believe it or not, it was sadly missing the daily routine of exercise! Our bodies are made to release endorphins, which improve our well-being and ability to cope. These are released through exercise. With this in mind, after a subdued Christmas, I braved the elements! It was tough at first, but slowly my stiff legs relaxed, my mind cleared and I realised just how much I had missed the countryside. New Year greetings were exchanged in all directions, reminding me how much running had introduced me to the neighbourhood and kept me in touch with the community. By the time I returned home, my attitude towards the marathon was transformed: I would go for it!

In order to build up the mileage towards the big 26.2 miles, I had to gradually increase to running 60 miles per week, and then slow down to a mere 40 miles per week for the fortnight preceding the big day. This was recovery time, in preparation for the 'real thing'! To fulfil my schedule, I ran whenever and wherever I could. My favourite time was first thing in the morning, but miles had to be made up in the evening and at midday. One memorable run, Doug accompanied me at midnight! My favourite place was when visiting the African country of Zambia. We ran through the streets of Ndola, joined by the laughing children, with their bright eyes and dazzling smiles.

With much trepidation, I entered the final ten weeks leading up to the London Marathon. Steve kindly drew up a training chart, which included three weeks of building endurance. Then came two weeks of concentrating on speed, followed by three tough weeks of final conditioning. Strangely, instead of feeling relief in the last two weeks of recovery, I felt I was wasting my time and losing ground. I longed to get on with it!

'What on earth are you running for?' was a question often asked by people in the early days when, like me, they viewed running as pointless and painful. Now the question came in a much more positive way. The runners in the marathon raise thousands of pounds for hundreds of charities and good causes. Family and friends wanted to join me in giving to whatever was on my heart. With my surprise acceptance into the marathon, and the tight schedule that resulted, I hadn't had time to think over the sponsoring and direction of giving. I replied with the first thing that came into my mind: the children of Beirut! During the war out in the Lebanon, Doug and our eldest son Steve had travelled to Beirut with the Saltmine Trust to visit schools and churches. Money needed to be raised to help children to have holidays from the war-torn city. They could be taken to Cyprus or Switzerland. My dream was to bring them to the south of England. Imagine my excitement when I heard that Terry Waite, the Archbishop of Canterbury's special envoy, was to start the marathon off. The Hezbollah had released him from captivity in the Lebanon just months before.

On the eve of the marathon, we travelled up to central London with the Poole runners in the comfort of a coach, and settled into a bed and breakfast. No amount of laughter and jokes could hide my apprehension. We all piled into a restaurant for what felt like my last meal, I was so nervous. This was 'pasta packing' time, ready for the long haul next day. Regardless of how I felt, my training locked in. I had to eat! After the first few mouthfuls, the delicious taste took over, and my anxiety receded with the good company. It returned in force as I lay in bed several hours later! We had to be up for a 6 am breakfast, so we wouldn't be running on full stomachs at the start of the race. You can imagine how this novice felt, having just force-fed myself on pasta, with the prospect of a full English breakfast in a few hours! The night eventually passed with little sleep, and the breakfast was surprisingly welcome and delicious!

As the thousands of runners converged onto Blackheath in south London for the start of this momentous marathon, the accumulative apprehension was almost tangible. Everyone seemed to be expert in their preparation. They were greasing their legs. So I greased my legs! They were stretching their muscles. So I stretched my muscles! In the end, I gave up watching others and made my way to my starting area, to indulge myself in outright panic! This was an amazing multitude of 'dustbin bag clad' athletes, striving to keep warm before the start. I searched over the heads of the other runners for a glimpse of the starting line, or the familiar figure of Terry Waite. Neither could be seen. The top athletes and wheelchair athletes were well into their race. An expectant hush fell on the thousands as 9.30 am drew near. My heartbeat was increasing with the excitement as the runners moved forward in anticipation.

As the signal resounded through the heath, I was swept along in such a massive wave of humanity that I never saw the starting line, let alone Terry Waite, who was cheering us through! The friendly banter from fellow runners, and the shouts and encouragement from the crowds, accompanied the pounding of thousands of trainers on the tarmac and the steady beat of the bands along the route. The worldwide support through the media was evident, as cameramen called for our attention and response. We were swept along on a tide of tension. As a result, when I completed the sixth mile, I was fit to drop! I had been running on excitement and had forgotten to pace myself! Slowing to a sedate jog, I gathered my concentration. I still had over 20 miles to cover, and desperately wanted to look as if I was coping when I reached Tower Bridge. This was the landmark approaching the halfway distance of 13.1 miles. Doug, Liz and other running friends were waiting to cheer me over the River Thames. This expectancy got me through the next six miles. As I swung round to cross the historic bridge, my eyes were raking the crowds to catch a glimpse of the familiar faces. I needed to see them first, in order to go up a gear and to disguise my weariness! Suddenly, there was Doug, jumping up and down like a demented duck! His shouts and encouragement got me across the bridge, but as I hit the other side of the Thames, I was devastated! Leaving those I loved behind emphasised my loneliness and magnified the further 13 miles I still had to run!

How quickly our lives can swing from the excitement of the start and new beginnings, to depression and discouragement when things don't run quite as we had expected. The teenager Joseph lived a life of dramatic highs and desperate lows that surely should have caused him to give up. His life's story commences in Genesis 37. The favourite son of a large family, he grows up loved and cared for. God speaks to him through dreams and prepares him for his future. What a start for a young man! But without warning, he hits the first wall.

Captured by his jealous brothers, he is stripped of his richly ornamented robe, a gift from his father, and sold as a slave into Egypt. He must have hit rock-bottom. But does he give up? No! He starts from the bottom and works up in the household of his new master, Potiphar, Pharaoh's captain of the guard. Because of his success, Potiphar puts him in charge of his whole household, and entrusts to his care everything he owns. From that moment on, all Joseph touches turns to gold. He is a handsome, respected young man, and has risen to the top again.

Wait for it! The next twist is just round the corner. The lady of the house, Potiphar's wife, has her eye on him. She tries to seduce him, but without success. In retaliation, she falsely accuses him of inappropriate behaviour. In a fury, her husband throws Joseph into prison. Instead of allowing self-pity and bitterness to cripple him, he picks himself up and starts the upward climb all over again!

Within the confines of prison, his conduct finds favour with the warder, and he is put in charge of all those held in the prison. He meets up with the king's cupbearer and baker, both in custody for offending Pharaoh. They share their dreams with him. Joseph gives them God's interpretation. Both dreams are fulfilled on the king's birthday. The cupbearer is restored to his service in the king's palace, and the baker is hanged! Joseph is still in for disappointment. Instead of representing Joseph before the king, as he promised, the reinstated servant forgets all about him! The two long years of silence that follow emphasise his feeling of abandonment.

I can almost hear my hurt, human reaction in a similar situation: 'That's the last time I give anyone the benefit of my gifting!' But not Joseph! Through this long, hard haul he keeps in touch with his guide. He listens to, and learns from, his God. This is very evident when he is summoned to the palace.

The cupbearer has eventually remembered him. As he listens to two dreams that Pharaoh is sharing, he is reminded of the wise interpretations of Joseph in prison. Joseph is summoned into the king's presence, and speaks God's answer to the meaning of the two dreams. After giving wise counsel in dealing with seven years of plenty, followed by seven years of famine, Pharaoh appoints Joseph as prime minister over Egypt, to guide them through the crisis.

From a teenager through to the age of 30, Joseph has been knocked down on numerous occasions. There are many more heartaches to come before he makes the great age of 110! How does he keep 'up and running'? The answer lies in the last chapter of Genesis (50:20–21). His teenage dream is fulfilled as his brothers throw themselves down before him as his slaves, pleading for his forgiveness. Joseph responds:

> You intended to harm me, but God intended it for good to accomplish what is now being done, the saving of many lives. So then, don't be afraid. I will provide for you and your children.

No way would Joseph have chosen the route he had been forced to take, but the tough thread of truth that holds him together in these 13 chapters is found in the continual reminder that 'the Lord was with Joseph'! In his brutal capture by his own brothers? The Lord was with Joseph! Sold as a slave into Egypt? The Lord was with Joseph! Wrongly accused by Potiphar's wife? The Lord was with Joseph! Thrown into prison? The Lord was with Joseph! Forgotten and ignored? The Lord was with Joseph! It's so easy to see the presence of the Lord and to praise him when Joseph becomes prime minister. Joseph survived both physically and spiritually, because he kept 'up and running' with the Lord, whatever walls he hit!

It seemed brutally different for me at this halfway stage of the marathon. This wall was far worse than I had expected. There seemed no point in my continuing when all around me were quitting! A voice in my head pleaded with me to stop: 'You don't have to do this. Give up.' My dilemma was: what should I do?

Stretching exercises

1. How can we prepare ourselves, in the good times, for the unexpected circumstances which knock us down? 'Pasta packing', in preparation for the long haul in the marathon, taught me the urgency for memorising Scripture. How can 'the word of Christ dwell in . . . [us] richly' (Colossians 3:16) in times of crisis if we haven't fed our minds and hearts with it?

2. Share what has helped or hindered you in and through specific low times. This can not only help those going through similar situations, but can also prepare others for what lies ahead.

3. Pray specifically for each other. If it helps you, use the powerful words of Scripture to penetrate your daily lives, i.e. 'Let the peace of Christ rule in your hearts . . . Let the word of Christ dwell in you richly' (Colossians 3:15–16). A visual aid can also motivate our prayers. I have a prayer board on my kitchen door to jog my prayer life into action throughout the day. Exchange photos or prayer requests that can go on a board, or some other strategic place, to encourage continued prayer for each other.

4. Read Psalm 46. This is a powerful passage for times of crisis! Select one or two verses which will help you now, or prepare you for some future need. Share these in twos, or in a larger group. By reading and talking about these verses, you are in fact meditating, chewing over their meaning and significance. Meditating should not be emptying the mind. It is exercising the mind.

5. Whether together or alone, exercise your mind further in memorising your chosen verse. Progress gradually to memorising other verses, or the whole psalm! You can have the Bible always with you when it is hidden in your heart!

LAP 9

Running Mad

Leaving Tower Bridge behind, hearts were heavy, heads hung low and feet shuffled. As Canary Wharf loomed large on the skyline, it was as if a great blanket of depression descended on the panting masses. Runners were grinding to a halt, some were crippled with cramp and others had collapsed. St John's men and women administered first aid as the majority struggled to just keep running! In the months preceding this desperate moment, I had been warned and prepared for such a crisis. No amount of advice can equip you for the effect of the accumulative exhaustion and despondency of the thousands. The friendly banter between runners was silenced, the spectators' shouting was strangely muffled as I retreated into a private world of pain!

As we penetrated further into the East End Dockland, the cockneys' support became loud and colourful! Being married to one of these unique Londoners, I would have, under normal circumstances, warmed to their articulate support and contagious humour: 'Come on, gal, pick up your "plates of meat"! We know what you're going through. Don't give up. Get on with it!' I could have cheerfully punched them! The aggravation got me through the next mile! A relaxed day out for these onlookers, with plenty of laughter and drink – how could they possibly know what I was going through? I had even struggled with the appearance of Simon Hughes, the MP for Bermondsey, on the south side of the river. His support was obviously appreciated by runners and spectators, but I had a problem! His quiet presence at the roadside only accentuated the desperate straits I was in! He was immaculate in a suit, shirt and tie. Striking in appearance, with not a hair out of place, whereas with my regular dowsing and drinking at water stations, I looked more like a scarecrow on the run!

Hitting the wall in the human race is more excruciating than in the London Marathon. We retreat from onlookers, wrestle with our private agonies, and struggle from one day to the next. People, observing our personal ordeals, try to understand and support. Some tentatively come up with such phrases as: 'We know what you're going through,' or 'Snap out of it,' or 'You've got to keep going!' The brutal facts are: we don't want to; we can't, and no one can possibly know what we are going through! This then adds guilt to our predicament as we remind ourselves that people are only trying to help.

'Run with perseverance', the second guideline in Hebrews 12:1 of our training manual, is easier said than 'run'! It could be just one more trite phrase inadequately offered, if we didn't know where it was coming from. Having discovered the down-to-earth practicality of the first guideline, 'Throw off everything that hinders', I decided to explore the relevance of this coaching tip: 'Let us run with perseverance the race marked out for us.'

The London Marathon is an incredible feat of organisation. Born in the heart and mind of the athlete Chris Brasher,
his vision has grown through the years to become one of the
biggest, most successful marathons in the world. The course
is carefully mapped out across the streets of London, with
drinking stations strategically placed at every mile along the
route. Police, medical experts and general helpers are all on
duty, their main job to encourage, guide and protect the
runners. Traffic is redirected for several hours, to allow the
participants clear roads and safe running in the heart of
the city. Care is even taken to soften the cobbled area
through the Tower of London, by carpeting the footpath
beneath the bridge. The Beefeaters, in their full regalia,
appear to be guarding the runners as well as the historic
Tower! So efficient is the organisation of this race that within
hours the city is returned to normal with not a trace of the
teeming thousands.

Our human race is far more breathtaking in its birth!
Ephesians 1:4 tells us we were in God's mind and heart
before the foundation of the world. It goes further to say:
'For he chose us in him before the creation of the world . . .'
Not only does God choose us, but he personally charts our
marathon. Every detailed direction and difficulty is there for
a reason. He is aware of every twist and turn, and feels each
pinpoint of pressure. A God who has not only run the race
before us, but has been cheered and jeered by the spectators,
understands our aggravation and annoyance. He is not a
distant, impersonal bystander, out for a day's entertainment;
he created this mighty marathon, and holds the secret to
completing it successfully. When he says, 'Run with perseverance,' he isn't just telling us to grit our teeth and do the
best we can. No! He is ready to supply us with the same

perseverance and endurance that broke through the wall of death on a Roman cross.

> . . . who for the joy set before him endured the cross, scorning its shame, and sat down at the right hand of the throne of God. Consider him who endured such opposition from sinful men, so that you will not grow weary and lose heart. (Hebrews 12:2–3)

We don't have to rely on periodic water stations. As we invite God our Creator into our personal marathon he brings all his resources to equip us. They are described in John 4:14 as 'the water I give . . . will become . . . a spring of water welling up to eternal life'. This is a life of quality as well as quantity. God's Spirit wants to fill us continually with all we need in our run through life. One memorable year, the temperature shot up unexpectedly into the 70s on the marathon day. Supplies of water ran out towards the end of the long race. However, God's supply never runs dry: the more we ask, the more he gives.

Back to the madness of the moment! Exaggerated by exhaustion, my annoyance with the crowds was soon forgotten when children offered carefully unwrapped sweets or segments of oranges to moisten my dry mouth. Bands played rhythmic music to accompany our running, and 'Keep right on to the end of the road' was sung raucously to encourage our waning strength.

It is not so easy to forget the anger and bitterness that naturally cramps us in the human race. Life is unfair! Sin has disfigured our race and the course we take. We can quickly become disillusioned and our strength runs out. One of the most effective pieces of training advice that pulled me through those tough miles in the marathon, and subsequent stretches in my human race, is found in Isaiah 40:31:

Those who hope in the Lord will renew their strength. They will soar on wings like eagles; they will run and not grow weary, they will walk and not be faint.

In my lowest times, I learnt to pound these words out as I weathered the tough miles. Because of the frequency of failing strength, they were well embedded into my mind, and I quickly experienced their staying power.

The example of the eagle is intriguing. What enables this powerful bird to weather hurricanes, and keep flying when all else is destroyed? The secret lies in the renewing of the feathers in their wings. God has created them in such an effective way that every feather is replaced, renewed, over several months each year! Their ability to manoeuvre, and appear nailed to the sky in hurricanes, is because of their powerful wings. Most birds are handicapped throughout this moulting and renewing process, but not the eagle. Owing to their need to survive in a tough environment, no two adjacent wing feathers moult at the same time. Bearing in mind that these mighty birds can have anything up to 7,182 feathers, this is a fantastic process to enable them to continue flight throughout!

This is how God wants to renew our strength, so that we can soar on wings like eagles! We can rise above the bitter blow of criticism, stay secure in the twister of torment, stand firm when the tornado of temptation hits us. When we feel hurtled off course by unforeseen squalls, he runs alongside us, steadies us and renews us. What an encouragement it is to read in Psalm 103:5: '[He] satisfies your desires with good things, so that your youth is renewed like the eagle's.'

Stretching exercises

1. What aggravates you most when the going gets tough?
2. Which person is most helpful at these times? Why do you think this is?
3. With the eagle in mind, how can we work with God in the renewing of our minds and hearts, as well as our strength? Memorise Isaiah 40:31.
4. Take a complete break for a day or a weekend with your group or a friend. If time only permits a few hours, guard this time for recharging your batteries. Discuss how best you can use this time to renew yourself and each other – e.g. recreation, Bible study, group activity.
5. Link the two guidelines from Hebrews 12:1 together, and memorise them: 'Let us throw off everything that hinders and the sin that so easily entangles, and let us run with perseverance the race marked out for us.'

LAP 10

Running Out of Time

I couldn't wait to fix my eyes on Big Ben! As I stumbled across the cobbled area through the Tower of London, beneath the bridge, the 20-mile goal was in sight! Instead of being encouraged by lasting out this long, I was reminded of the six plus miles that still lay ahead.

My first introduction to the marathon was when the final route to the finish lay along the Embankment, up through Trafalgar Square, under Admiralty Arch and down the Mall. It then swung left past Buckingham Palace, along Birdcage Walk and into Parliament Square. The last yards stretched past the House of Commons, with Big Ben towering above, to finish halfway across Westminster Bridge. Distorted in my weary mind, this seemed like another full-blown marathon! My long training runs had prepared me for the 20-mile distance. I was now breaking new ground! Leading up to the marathon, I was wisely advised not to exhaust myself with the full length, but to work up towards it for the big day.

Remembering what I had learnt about not looking too far ahead, I just coped with negotiating lampposts and trees as I ran along the Thames Embankment. Doug had crossed London on the Underground, and appeared suddenly on the roadside. I had no energy left to hide my fatigue – my eyes showed my true feelings!

Trafalgar Square distracted me briefly. I had learnt to drive in this capital city, and was used to the continual surge of several lanes of traffic. It was a unique experience of power to run in the centre of those roads, through red traffic lights, waved on by the police! This momentary release from tension swept me over the Square, under the Arch and onto the Mall. The length and width of this famous approach to Buckingham Palace filled me with renewed despair. In comparison I shrank into my narrow, short, quitting mentality. With desperation, my eyes raked the skyline for that famous clock. Its towering presence would assure me the end was in sight. Its welcoming chimes would have been sufficient, but there was neither sight nor sound of Big Ben. The statue of Queen Victoria looked down with a stony stare from her privileged seat outside the Palace. Eventually emerging from Birdcage Walk, I nearly fell into Parliament Square. The sudden sight of the clock filled my vision. The effect of running for well over four hours magnified the minute hand, and it seemed to hover just two minutes before two o'clock. My first goal, to complete the course, was now in sight and possible. With my eyes fixed on the clock, I realised time was running out for my second goal. As the minute hand moved annoyingly closer to the hour, I had less than 60 seconds to break my four-and-a-half hour deadline! My 'short, sharp bursting' mentality locked in, and the most memorable part of my marathon was the sprint across Westminster Bridge to cross the line in 4 hours 29 minutes and 48 seconds! As the historic clock chimed the hour of 2 pm across the city, I wanted to hug everyone in sight! I'd done it – run through the walls, overcome the obstacles, fought the fatigue, and hadn't run out of time!

In the human race, time is always running out. From the moment we are born, the minutes tick away incessantly. Our eyes are constantly on the clock, the calendar or the lap top organiser. Phrases such as: 'I haven't got the time', 'Give me a moment', and 'Where's the time gone?' highlight the transience of this valuable commodity. The mirror magnifies the passing of time as we fix our eyes on human appearance and personal achievement. God, however, has a sovereign time-table. He is not limited to time and 'has also set eternity in the hearts of men' (Ecclesiastes 3:11). He created us to live life to the full and to live for ever. Sin set the time bomb of death ticking!

Big Ben motivated me to achieve a transient goal, but where do I set my sights to cross over the final ribbon of this life? Our third and final guideline from Hebrews 12:2 is the answer:

> Let us fix our eyes on Jesus, the author and perfecter of our faith, who for the joy set before him endured the cross, scorning its shame, and sat down at the right hand of the throne of God.

We are urged not just to casually look at him, but to consider him, to think carefully about and meditate on him. Jesus was God made man, and limited to the time schedules of this world. His earthly life lasted 33 short years. As we follow his life here on earth through the Gospels, we observe no sin at all. He did not have to die; he chose to die, to diffuse the 'time bomb' and destroy the power of death: 'For God so loved the world that he gave his one and only Son, that whoever believes in him shall not perish but have eternal life' (John 3:16).

As I follow in my personal guide's footsteps in relationship with him, I can say to him, 'My times are in your hands.' David learnt and shared this in Psalm 31:15. God has perfect timing, and we can rest secure in his running schedule.

Time was running out for a widow and her only son in Zarephath of Sidon. Desperation had set in as she collected wood for a fire to prepare their last meal. To aggravate the situation, a man interrupted her stick-collecting, requesting water and food. Drought and famine had ravaged the land for years and all supplies had run out. Tears were not far away as she said:

'I don't have any bread – only a handful of flour in a jar and a little oil in a jug. I am gathering a few sticks to take home and make a meal for myself and my son, that we may eat it – and die.' (1 Kings 17:12)

Here is a perfect example of God's timing and provision. The man requesting the food is the marathon runner Elijah, God's prophet. God has told him to go at once to Zarephath. Without hesitation, he obeys immediately, and meets the widow at the gate of the town. In response to her plight, he reassures her: 'Don't be afraid. Go home and do as you have said. But first make a small cake of bread for me . . . and then make something for yourself and your son.' My patience would have been running out at this point, and I doubt whether I would have stayed to hear any more! I am so thankful for the widow's staying power, as Elijah's next words are the answer for their survival:

'This is what the Lord, the God of Israel, says: "The jar of flour will not be used up and the jug of oil will not run dry until the day the Lord gives rain on the land".'

Their time wasn't up; their provisions didn't run out, but it needed the trusting obedience of a widow to come to the rescue in following God's instructions. As we take our eyes off our selfish goals and ourselves, God gives us an entirely new perspective. When we first glimpse the widow, her eyes are downcast, concentrating on the dirty task of collecting wood. Her mind is centred on starvation and death. As she listens to God through his servant Elijah, her eyes are lifted out of the hollow of hunger, into the hope of a hot meal. The fear of death is replaced by a fresh new life for her and her son.

Our human race produces numerous 'laps' when we feel and know we are running out of time! Exams, careers, finding the right partner, reaching the top in our jobs, striving for the best and growing older are just a few. How can we prevent the panic of passing years, and invest time in God's agenda? A time-saving instruction found in Proverbs 3:5-6 is vital: 'Trust in the Lord with all your heart and lean not on your own understanding; in all your ways acknowledge him, and he will make your paths straight.' Our own understanding is so limited. God, who knows every step of our human race, wants to train us in leaning on his wisdom and guidance. He can pace us perfectly through the years and milestones of our life, and as we consult him, he will keep us on the right track. With God's everlasting life within us, and his Spirit guiding us, our time will never run out.

Stretching exercises

1. Share some of the goals you have achieved throughout your life (e.g. learning a musical instrument).

2. What or who motivated you to keep trying?

3. Share about some of the people who have been an inspiration in your human race for perseverance. Clare, my friend and prayer partner, has cerebral palsy. She drives, attends classes and participates wherever possible in our church activities. There is no sense of self-pity, and her gift of encouragement is very much appreciated.

4. How can we fix our eyes on Jesus, whom we cannot see physically? (For example, try to see him in your mind's eye, through reading the Bible.)

5. Name some areas in which you can waste time, e.g. television, gossip.

6. We are all in need of 'tips' on how to save time. Exchange ideas on what helps you to use your time well.

7. Memorise Ephesians 5:15–16: 'Be very careful, then, how you live – not as unwise but as wise, making the most of every opportunity, because the days are evil.' Making the most of every opportunity is translated in the Authorised Version as 'redeeming the time'. God enables us to 'buy back' our time as we use it with and for him.

LAP 11

Running with the Story

Wrapped in tin foil immediately after completing the marathon, I felt like a turkey ready for the oven. Munching an energy-replacing bar of chocolate and swigging water like there was no tomorrow, we were guided to our own personal lorries to find our clothes. Tracksuits and equipment we shed at the beginning of the marathon had been driven across London for us to pick up at the end. Juggling with the heavy marathon medal placed round my neck, I changed my clothes and hurried to the prearranged meeting point with Doug. Runners were exchanging stories about their past hours of effort, and officials were constantly congratulating us. The pain of the 'long haul' was quickly forgotten as friends and family were found and regaled with every little detail of the experience. Doug listened patiently to my excited ramblings until I sank, exhausted, into my seat on the train. This was my first free ride, because of my medal, on the London Underground! As the 'tube' hurtled through the tunnel, I closed my eyes and vowed never to run another step.

My underground vow was forgotten the very next day! After a long night of sleep, I emerged onto the roads of Christchurch, unable to keep the story to myself. I readily stopped to answer the neighbourhood's questions about the 'big day'. Many had watched the bobbing heads filling their television screens. No one had seen me, but nothing could spoil the incredible story I was running with. I hadn't hit the headlines, or made the nine o'clock news. The event would be forgotten tomorrow by the media, but no one could take away from me the memory of my first marathon. For several days, I was running on a high. Senses were heightened and emotions were fragile. Music and memories would trigger the tears and it was very difficult to stop talking about every little detail of the race. After the publishing of our names in *The Times* newspaper with our finishing times, the memory started to recede. I had to get on with my human race, with its continual demands of family, work and home.

How quickly stories are dropped by the media. Today's eye-catching headlines are tomorrow's recycling bundles. There is, however, one story that has continued to run down through the ages. It has withstood the rejection of the media and outrun the fleeting bigger stories. It has sold record-breaking copies of its book and has changed the whole destination of the human race. 'For the wages of sin is death, but the gift of God is eternal life in Christ Jesus our Lord' (Romans 6:23). For 2,000 years this story of hope has not left the headlines. It has been ignored or forgotten, but has never stopped running. Jesus, the central figure, is fulfilling his every promise, unlike many figures in the media, and thousands are discovering his powerful input into their human race. Why am I not running with this life-changing story in the same way that I couldn't hold back on my marathon sharing? The need to introduce our 'personal Sweeper' Jesus Christ to fellow runners in our human race has never been more urgent.

I was seven years old and running as fast as my little legs would carry me. My dad had just been swept up by a gigantic wave and thrown onto a concrete breakwater in Brighton, and our family holiday had been thrown into turmoil! As we huddled around him on the beach, blood poured from his nose. My sisters and I were sent in both directions along the promenade to find a Red Cross station. Bursting unannounced into the beach hut, I gasped my plea for help! Registering my concern and urgency, two experts jumped up, grabbed their medical cases and ran with me back along the beach, listening to my story. I can't have made much sense, being a child and out of breath, but I shall always be thankful for their immediate response. After the treatment had been given to my father and he had been admitted to hospital, the first aid personnel told my mother that they hadn't understood too much of what I had said, but had seen in my face and urgent running that action was needed immediately. The love and concern that I felt for my father was matched by the urgency with which I ran. I believed his life was at risk! We are running with a story for friends and family whose lives are at risk! I am so thankful that the verse in Romans 6:23 doesn't finish with death, but comes up with the solution: '. . . but the gift of God is eternal life in Christ Jesus our Lord.'

Later on in life, I was to learn from another of God's runners in Acts 8:4–8, 26–40. We don't read that Philip is a marathon runner, or even a regular jogger, but there is urgency about his sprint in verse 30. He has just had two directions from his personal 'Sweeper', the Holy Spirit. The fact that he has heard both instructions and acted on them proves how closely he sticks to his guide. 'Go south to the road – the desert road – that goes down from Jerusalem to Gaza' (v. 26).

Philip has been running a massive mission in a city in Samaria. His preaching, teaching, healing and delivery ministry must have left him drained and in need of rest. Yet, as soon as he hears God's direction, he acts immediately. He withdraws from the crowds and the city and makes his way down a desert road. Like a blind runner, he does not know where this path will lead him, but trusts implicitly his 'all-seeing guide'. No sooner has he acted on the first 'clue' in this divine treasure hunt than he receives his next one. As a line of chariots suddenly confronts him, God says: 'Go to that chariot and stay near it' (v. 29).

He responds with an urgency that causes him to run, and an accuracy that takes him to the exact chariot containing the specific Ethiopian eunuch that the Holy Spirit is already working in. We have an expert team runner in the Holy Spirit. He is not only within us and alongside us, but also out ahead of us, working in the hearts of those specific people he is going to bring across our track to share with them the story we are running with.

Liz, who introduced me to running, was a classic example of this. On one of the first Sundays I was able to attend my home church after much travelling and speaking, I was looking forward to a rest. The service drew to a close, and we moved through to the lounge for a welcome cup of coffee. Unlike Philip, I was not consciously listening for God's direction. I made for an empty table with my coffee. Liz had visited our church for the first time that day; she had just made that first hesitant step of commitment, and urgently needed to understand what it was all about. Seeing me, a stranger, at an empty table was the opportunity she needed. God used my tiredness, and need to be alone, to set up a divine appointment, which not only introduced Liz to some spiritual training sessions, but started me on the marathon path! God has a sense of humour! He wants us to run with his story, aware that he is opening up the opportunities. He doesn't want us running around like headless chickens, frantically talking to anyone and everyone, and plunging into a guilt trip when we haven't witnessed to at least ten people each day! I learnt a powerful lesson that Sunday morning: God can use our weariness in witnessing, our loneliness in listening, and our shyness in sharing.

Philip shows us the importance of listening. His urgent run could have automatically interrupted the eunuch's reading of the book of Isaiah the prophet. He grinds to a halt and listens to the prophetic words about Jesus in Isaiah 53:7–8:

> He was led like a sheep to the slaughter, and as a lamb before the shearer is silent, so he did not open his mouth. In his humiliation he was deprived of justice. Who can speak of his descendants? For his life was taken from the earth.

Philip starts right where that Ethiopian is. He answers his questions and runs with the story being read: 'Then Philip began with that very passage of Scripture and told him the good news about Jesus' (v. 35).

Stretching exercises

1. In twos, share a personal story that really excites you. (For me, an example is learning to ski when I was halfway to 90!)
2. Think of headlines that have made the news and have now been dropped.
3. Create headlines you would like to see across our papers, relating to the 2000-year-old story of Jesus.
4. Relate a childhood incident that caused you to run with an urgency, e.g. races at school, or running home with the results of exams, if they were good!
5. Share your own personal Jesus story: how you first met him, and who helped you. If you find this difficult, write it out first, and then read it. It is a good exercise for everyone to capture on paper this miracle meeting. Writing always helps us communicate more clearly.
6. Highlight people who have crossed your path in life, asking questions. How did you answer them? I learnt quickly with Liz not to pretend I had all the answers. She came up with all the 'toughies'. Our weekly group, which had then grown to four, would go home for some research, and return the following week with ideas and answers.
7. Memorise 1 Peter 3:15: 'Always be prepared to give an answer to everyone who asks you to give the reason for the hope that you have.' Writing out your testimony helps you to be prepared.

LAP 12

Running in Tandem

Distance can glamorise and colour memories of a marathon. Very different the cold light of 8 am! No longer alone, I gasped my way around Hengistbury Head and back along the River Stour to Christchurch, urged on by a maddeningly energetic husband!

Isolation, the image of running that had caused me to avoid it in the early days, was now strangely attractive to me. I had become accustomed to solitude and the sound of silence. Since Doug has been running, he is stronger and faster than I am. No longer can I 'trundle' and dream. He nags and cajoles, calling it encouragement and pacing! His long-distance, methodical mentality challenges my spasmodic, impulsive bursts of speed. Gradually, I have grown to rely on his presence just a few steps ahead. As he draws away, I strain to keep in touch, until, catching up with him, the rhythm of our united footsteps keeps me going and 'ups' my pace.

We set off on our 'marriageathon' 37 years ago. The walls

we have hit individually and together could have blown us apart. There were times when we struggled to keep going, through misunderstanding, failure and sheer fatigue. Our disposable society crushes, recycles and replaces most things, including, sadly, relationships. For any marriage to survive, it needs sacrificial 'long-distance' commitment. It requires a determination not to give up at the first 'wall', and the next, and the next! A willingness to find a way through, by pooling resources, not piling resentment.

The 'urge to merge' is irresistible! Marriage is like the joining of two mighty rivers. We should not have been surprised at the turbulent waters that resulted. The differences we discovered in our running together were only a faint shadow of the contrasting characters, upbringings, experiences, strengths and weaknesses that vie for position in this human relationship. Doug's river had its origin in the tough East End of London. As a child, he experienced the trauma of the Second World War, with the concentration of bombing on the Docklands. The working classes toughed it out with all hands on deck, dads and mums working from dawn until dusk to survive! Doug, the eldest son, shared a bed with his two brothers until he was 18; his sister's bed was alongside – a family of six, in three rooms, with another family upstairs. The East End community spirit, centred on the family and the pub, united them against all odds, and brought Doug through the choppy waters to his teens.

Four years after Doug, I was born in south London. I was the third of four daughters in a middle-class family, where all the men, including my father, had disappeared to fight for their country. We had a four-bedroom house, with a mum full time at home, and grandparents and aunts in plenty. Our extended family was a lively, caring church; a security I have come to understand and appreciate more as the years have gone by.

So here we have two London families of six – air raid sirens a familiar sound, search lights raking the night skies! There the similarity ends. Our upbringing might as well have been poles apart! Contrasting childhoods can pile resentment higher than a hurdle and wider than a wall, if not shared and understood. Built-in reactions and responses stem from early experiences. As we merge in marriage, the closeness magnifies our contrasting approaches to life. They are not necessarily wrong – they are just different!

Take my mother, for example. Laughter was a precious legacy given me by her through the tough war years. This sense of humour followed me through my teens and developed a positive approach to the most trying times, recognising the amusing side to most situations. Coming from a medical family, my approach to crisis followed my mother's example. Her laughter diffused the tension and stress, and created a 'short cut' to the real issue and need. Falling headfirst down steep stairs at the age of seven at our south London home should have been traumatic. My clearest memory of it was laughing in my mother's arms on the floor at the foot of the stairs. I realise now she would always be checking that there were no bones broken, and if there was an emergency, her reassuring voice always replaced the laughter. My training as a physical education teacher added to my calm approach to the unexpected.

Several miles across London, Doug was enjoying a completely different maternal management of accidents: everything ground to a desperate halt when any member of the family was hurt. Hours of urgent, serious attention were given, and the whole neighbourhood would rally round. Just imagine how my new husband felt when, shortly after our wedding day, he was trying out his DIY skills. Wielding a hammer, he thundered it down on his finger instead of the nail he was holding. He was met with shrieks of laughter as I applied the first aid. He saw me as an insensitive, thoughtless woman who didn't care! My response to his moody silence was that he was immature and wanting too much attention. For a number of years, we just observed one another in these crisis situations, not understanding the background from which our reactions had grown. This sounds a mild misunderstanding in human relationship, but, allowed to fester, resentment grows out of all recognition and can destroy a marriage.

'Bloat', a dangerous condition in cattle, illustrates this perfectly. If a cow eats the wrong kind of food, it will fester in its stomach and expel toxic gases, causing its stomach to swell up dangerously. Unless an expert is called in to pierce the animal's stomach in just the right place in order to release this poison, the animal will die. The same can happen with resentment, impatience and misunderstanding. Fed into our minds and hearts, they can 'bloat' the tiniest details out of all proportion, and destroy relationships. I needed to look beneath Doug's approach to crisis, and he needed to see through my laughter. By reminiscing, we recalled our two mothers' different characters and responses, and soon realised that the two extremes needed to be merged and adjusted in our family.

Running highlighted another area in our marriage that required understanding. Doug has an incredible in-built sense of direction. Through many months of lone running, I had learned training routes by getting lost! My love for breaking new ground gave many creative opportunities for finding my way through tough terrain that Doug would have sensibly found an alternative route to avoid. I was so thankful that he

wasn't with me when I ended up knee deep in mud on the wet
sandy heathland of the Avon Valley! What a difference his
forward planning and direction made when training for my
second marathon. I did, however, miss those spontaneous,
pioneering adventures, when I took off for 'who knows where'
and discovered new routes and hidden trails. Doug needs to
know the end from the beginning! He must have a clear
picture in mind of the entire project before setting out. He
sums up the advantages and disadvantages, the positives and
negatives, and thrives on training charts and schedules. In retrospect, debating and discussing the full picture of my first
'asthmatic run round the block' with Liz would have nipped
in the bud any thoughts of running the marathon. In the
human race, and particularly when 'running in tandem', both
techniques are necessary. The immediate needs and challenges
should be balanced, where possible, with long-term planning
and wise sense of direction. Finances, children, employment
and housing all require instant, spontaneous decisions,
coupled with 'long-distance' perspective and guidance.

I am thankful we cannot see the full course of our human
race. If I had known in advance some of the walls I would
have to run through, I would have quit long ago, and have
missed out on the lessons learnt through the tough times! The
only person who knew the end from the beginning was Jesus!
From the moment he donned the 'human strip', his course
was destined for the cross! However, it was because of what
lay after the cross that he kept on running: '. . . who for the joy
set before him endured the cross, scorning its shame, and sat
down at the right hand of the throne of God' (Hebrews 12:2).

At first reading, this verse suggests that Jesus couldn't wait
to get back home to his Father. The incredible discovery I made
with deeper reading is that you and I are all a vital part of the

joy etched in the mind of Jesus that motivated him to break through the wall of death. He longed to see us united with him, and the price that had to be paid for that was his life sacrificed on the cross. I couldn't wait to see Doug at the completion of the first gruelling 26.2 miles I ran. He had always believed I could do it, and was there for me through thick and thin. No one was there for Jesus! His best friends deserted him in fear of their own lives. Cheering crowds from his triumphant arrival in Jerusalem now bayed for his blood, crying, 'Crucify him! Crucify him!' Even his Father had to abandon his one and only Son because of the sin that was weighing him down. This was the darkest, loneliest, most excruciating marathon of all time, and he went through it for me!

From the sixth hour until the ninth hour darkness came over all the land. About the ninth hour Jesus cried out in a loud voice, '*Eloi, Eloi, lama sabachthani*?' – which means, 'My God, my God, why have you forsaken me?' (Matthew 27:45–46)

The name of Jesus raises a major contrast and similarity in Doug's and my background. We were both familiar with the name very early on in our childhood. My hearing and use of it was through bedside prayers, Sunday school, hymns and the Bible. For Doug, it was a natural part of East End vocabulary, in times of annoyance, anger, surprise and pain. We grew up with it, but for each of us it was just a word, sometimes a picture, and a good excuse for presents at Christmas and chocolate eggs at Easter. Long before our first meeting, we separately had an encounter with the living Jesus. For Doug, it was a sudden confrontation with the facts of the Resurrection, and the recognition that Jesus was alive today. His decision to not only accept the facts, but to step out in faith with a living God, changed the whole course of his life! For me, it was very different. The familiar name of Jesus became an embarrassment to me in my teens, as I tried to avoid it, not knowing why. It was a gradual realisation, over two years, that going to church and knowing 'about' Jesus wasn't enough. The reason for my embarrassment was that the living Lord Jesus was gradually making himself known to me personally. As a teenager always on the go, he was trying to grab my attention. This running away from a 'name' continued for two confused years, until I was confronted with his living words from Revelation:

> Listen! I stand at the door and knock; if anyone hears my voice and opens the door, I will come in and eat with them, and they will eat with me. (Revelation 3:20 GNB)

In responding to a living person, I changed the whole direction of my running. Inviting Jesus into my human race, I was now running with him, not away from him. Ours were two entirely different routes to the same Jesus. Several years later, our courses converged, and now we are running in tandem both in the marriageathon and the marathon!

Following my first marathon, 40 children, plus ten workers, were brought over from the Lebanon to spend three weeks of holiday, activity and teaching in Christchurch, Dorset. So much was learnt by all of us through this time together that we longed to repeat the venture, hence the running together round Hengistbury Head. We had both been accepted for the London Marathon this time, and needed to clock up the miles! Our goal was to break the four-hour timing, which would cut my previous running time by half an hour! This was serious training. Running alone had allowed me to use the exercise as a time to unwind and get things into perspective. My thoughts were often not on the running, but on sorting out problems and analysing situations. With Doug pacing me, I had to be focused, and was running much faster.

The regular exercise had transformed Doug. Much of his life and work had been stationary, studying at a desk, sitting at the wheel of a car, or standing in a pulpit, speaking. The running improved his health and also refreshed his mind. His communication, humour and contact with people suggest Doug is the typical cockney extrovert. He is, however, essentially a very private man, who rarely verbalises concerns, but mulls over them. In contrast, I would rabbit on about anything and everything, shedding my anxiety, often at his expense! Running together silenced me, and released him! He was able to talk up, and I learnt to shut up! Love is completing, not competing. Running together strangely accelerated this process!

We were into our last week of training. The big day loomed large on the horizon. Working up to the 60 mile per week schedule had seen us running in all kinds of weather. One memorable morning, we had braved rain, hail, thunder and lightning, all blown together by a biting wind, which seemed to come from all directions! In preparation for the 'long haul', all conditions have to be faced. Fair weather running is not sufficient. After the winter months of training, you can imagine our relief to wake up on the marathon morning in our 'home' city of London to sunshine! Spirits were high as we travelled to the 'start', packed like sardines into the underground trains! Spilling out onto Blackheath, there was little time for panic as we made our way to the starting area. Watches were being checked, muscles stretched, as we impatiently awaited the start of this epic race. I recognised the uncanny hush that slowly engulfed the waiting thousands, listening for the signal that would set this massive sea of humanity rolling! As our eyes met, Doug and I realised there was no turning back now. The signal sounded, and we were off!

Stretching exercises

1. Define some of the different relationships we have in life (e.g. work, team, marriage).
2. Describe your background and upbringing. It might help to write it down if you have painful memories.
3. How has this helped or hindered your building of friendships? (For instance, the example of my mother coping with people in crisis.)
4. Which person in your life has taught you the most about building lasting relationships? Can you highlight how they did this?
5. Thinking of the Snoopy cartoons entitled 'Love is . . .', invent your own personal definition (For example, 'Love is building up, not knocking down.')
6. How can we prepare and 'train' ready for the tough times in our relationships? (For example, talking and praying things through.)
7. Memorise John 15:12–13: 'My command is this: Love each other as I have loved you. Greater love has no-one than this, that he lay down his life for his friends.' This is Jesus speaking of his death, but what are some of the practical ways we can lay down our lives for our friends in this present day and age (e.g. giving our time)?

LAP 13

Running a Temperature

We had been running for three hours, and were on target for breaking our four hour goal. The crowds had multiplied since my last marathon, packing the pavements and spilling into the roads. The atmosphere was electrifying, with more bands playing and louder voices urging us on. Doug's presence alongside me, or just a few steps ahead, was an encouragement among the 'swarming hoards'! As we hit tough patches we weren't alone, and helped each other through them.

For part of the way we had run alongside a group of men who had run in the 100th Boston marathon just the week before. It wasn't long before they left us behind! The Tower of London was our next landmark and, as I approached it, I glanced to my side for Doug's reassurance. There was no sign of him! I searched the heads in front of me, and then swung round to rake through the faces behind. His familiar figure had disappeared! I knew he wouldn't have left me behind, and I stopped in agitation. 'What's the matter, love? Can we

95

help?' The spectators are always supportive, and they listened to my description of Doug, ready to search for him! Suddenly, I caught sight of him stumbling towards me. The temperature had rocketed into the 70s since the start of the race. Drinks were running out, and many runners had fallen by the wayside. This was a huge contrast to our recent outing through hail, thunder and lightning. The heat was on, and Doug had sunstroke!

For months, Doug had been out front, leading, motivating and inspiring. A shadow of his former self, he now peered at me through vague eyes and draped his arm around me for support. 'You go on,' he gasped. 'You can break the four hours!' His head was pounding, his temperature was soaring, and his legs were buckling. No way was I going to leave him. Slowly, we made our way to the next drinking station and took on more water, sponging his head and neck. Taking the next mile at a gentle walk, his strength began to return. The throbbing in his head receded, and his temperature returned to normal. Gradually he quickened his pace and we were on the run again!

*   *   *

Stripped of all my security, I lay alone on the floor of our now bare living-room, trying to sleep. A massive removal van held the furniture and belongings that we had accumulated over the last twelve years. All that was left was me and Nibbles, the black and white rabbit! Our eleven- and nine-year-old sons were staying with friends while we moved, and Doug had just been rushed into hospital with internal bleeding from a duodenal ulcer. Happy memories seemed to have been wiped out as our home was stripped and Doug had collapsed. I no longer belonged there, and was stepping out alone into the unknown. I desperately wanted to stay near Doug, who needed instant surgery, but knew I must oversee the move from London down to the south coast, before I returned to his side. The heat was rising, and the pressure of circumstances was closing in from all directions! How do we keep going when we hit walls like these in our human race?

Paul the apostle, who endured persecution, imprisonment and eventually death for his faith, says in 2 Corinthians 1:8:

> We were under great pressure, far beyond our ability to endure, so that we despaired even of life. Indeed, in our hearts we felt the sentence of death. But this happened that we might not rely on ourselves but on God . . .

How did Paul cope, after his conversion, with all that life threw at him? The answer lies in the same letter that he wrote to the church in Corinth:

> We are hard pressed on every side, but not crushed; perplexed, but not in despair; persecuted, but not abandoned; struck down, but not destroyed . . . Therefore we do not lose heart. Though outwardly we are wasting away, yet inwardly we are being renewed day by day. (2 Corinthians 4:8–9, 16)

We can keep our 'cool' when the heat is on, when we rely on the renewing power of God the Holy Spirit.

As a child, I used to think the height of maturity was to stand at an ironing board doing the ironing! I studied my mother's swinging, thumping action as the linen sizzled under her pressure and the steam escaped into the air. I longed to follow her example, but strangely was never allowed to! One memorable evening, my mother was drawing to the close of a marathon iron. All that was left was a pile of handkerchiefs, tray cloths and a few socks. As the massive pile of laundry was being taken up to the airing cupboard, I pleaded for permission to finish off the last few pieces. Seated on a high stool I was allowed to fulfil my dream! Carefully copying my mum, the iron was pressed firmly down on one side of the first handkerchief, all moisture hissing its way out from the heavy pressure. As if this wasn't enough I flipped the hanky over and started all over again on the other side! My childlike mind started to imagine how the hanky felt. Its yelps of pain and frustration could almost be heard in my imagination, as the heat and pressure continually came from all directions.

I have to admit, I cried like a child that night on the floor of our empty home. The pressure was coming from all directions, and it was too hot for comfort. The letter from Paul reminds us: 'We are hard pressed on every side, but not crushed.' In retrospect, when God allows pressure beyond our control, he uses it to iron out our awkward edges. He smoothes out our creased lives to make them more effective for him and those around us. I still prefer a smooth, soft linen handkerchief to a rough tissue for my sore, runny nose!

When I'd finished ironing the handkerchief, I then grabbed what looked like a piece of rag ready for the bin! As I spread it out and slowly applied the heat and pressure, the most beautiful, hand-sewn, pure white tray cloth emerged. My little eyes couldn't believe it! My grandmother had spent hours working intricately on this cloth, and it was only useful once ironed. The heat of the moment can cause us to be perplexed, or 'screwed up' like the tray cloth. With God in control of the divine pressure, Paul has the answer: 'We are . . . perplexed, but not in despair', because we are told in Psalm

139:13, 'For you created my inmost being; you knit me together in my mother's womb.' The tough times directed by, and accepted from, God are necessary to enable us to reach our full potential – like the tray cloth, to be used for what we were made for.

I was nearing the end of my task. My mother was still sorting out the airing cupboard, so I set to work on the heap of socks. Pairing them up carefully, I piled them neatly to the side. There was one lonely sock left! Down through the years, I have always had this problem. Where do all the odd socks go? As a child, I felt sorry for this lost sock, and searched for its partner. With three men in my life, I have long lost the fascination with both ironing and odd socks! There have been many times when I have felt like that odd sock: abandoned, not belonging, or left out and useless. That lonely night in between homes, with Doug and the boys elsewhere, my emotions were fragile, and I felt desolate. God is the only person who will never leave us whatever the circumstances, as Paul proved, 'We are . . . persecuted, but not abandoned'.

The ironing was finished, and still my mother hadn't appeared. I knew only too well the procedure of putting the iron and board away. I had watched often enough in admiration as my mum had thumped the legs in place and stood the ironing board in the cupboard. Enjoying my new-found independence, I unplugged the iron and put it in its usual place to cool. Having jumped off the stool, I now surveyed the ironing board from my six-year-old perspective. This was exciting. I followed what my mother always did. I placed one hand at one end of the board. Lifting it very slowly, because it was much heavier than I thought, I banged the legs with the other hand. It all happened too quickly. With a mighty crash, the full weight trapped my fingers, and I fell beneath the board onto the ground. The sound I heard was not my mother's laughter this time. I shall always remember the pounding of her feet on the stairs as she ran to my cry for help.

Paul knew what it was to be 'struck down, but not destroyed'. We find the reason in Hebrews 2:18: 'Because he himself suffered when he was tempted, he is able to help those who are being tempted'. We see again that powerful word, rooted in the Greek, 'help'. It means literally that Jesus will run to our cry. Here is our 'personal Sweeper' again, responding to our needs and running alongside to help. He knows all about the crushing of Gethsemane and the cross. He was despised and abandoned, wrongly accused and struck down, but never destroyed. He has the secret to running through the most pressurised times.

It was a new experience for me to be supporting and encouraging Doug in this second marathon. I also had to adjust to a new route to finish. Running the full-length of the Embankment up to Big Ben, we were now turning away from my previous final goal. Running across Parliament Square, we approached Buckingham Palace along Birdcage Walk. The final sprint to the finishing line was halfway up the Mall towards Trafalgar Square. After all the heat and strain, we still broke my previous time by five-and-a-half minutes: 4 hours 24 minutes 10 seconds. We proved the words from Isaiah 40:31:

> But those who hope in the Lord will renew their strength. They will soar on wings like eagles; they will run and not grow weary, they will walk and not be faint.

Stretching exercises

1. Define some of the pressures we face today, e.g. peer pressure, exams.
2. Share, or write down, a crisis time in your life that has caused temperatures to rise.
3. Memorise 2 Corinthians 4:8–9, 16:

   > We are hard pressed on every side, but not crushed; perplexed, but not in despair; persecuted, but not abandoned; struck down, but not destroyed . . . Therefore we do not lose heart. Though outwardly we are wasting away, yet inwardly we are being renewed day by day.

4. Share practical ways of coping with pressure, e.g. listening to music, running, praying with a friend.
5. Share specific lessons you have learnt as a direct result of tough times, e.g. dependence on God rather than others.
6. Revise Isaiah 40:31, memorised after Lap 9:

   > But those who hope in the Lord will renew their strength. They will soar on wings like eagles; they will run and not grow weary, they will walk and not be faint.

LAP 14

Running on the Edge

One false step and I would have plunged up to 1,500 feet to the valley and tarn below. Testing each crevice first, I made my precarious way down rocks and scree from the summit of Helvellyn onto Striding Edge. My heart was in my mouth as I surveyed the 300 yard long narrow spine of rock, sculptured by ice and storm. This stark, bony arm is one of two protruding from the Helvellyn summit to encircle the silent waters of the Red Tarn in its valley.

We had spent two hours climbing the 3,148 feet from Wythburn to the famous fell summit, to view Striding Edge. Momentarily, I was regretting every step as the panic of 'striding the Edge' became a definite reality, not a distant locality! I had been warned, and where possible prepared, for this climbing expedition, but no words could describe those hours spent the day before scrambling, clinging, tripping, sliding and very briefly running on the Edge! The breathtaking beauty surrounding us was forgotten as we struggled to keep our grip on the rocky crag. It was a 'stomach churning' journey in the Lake District I shall always remember.

The accelerated pace and the demands of life today cause us to scale the heights of others' expectations of us, and our own desire to succeed. All that the media and society promise never seems to satisfy, and we continue to climb, vainly searching for fulfilment and clinging to our hopes, which are continually shaken by our fears.

'Running on the edge' was a perfect description of me when our two lads had just started school. Now was the time for me to use my training as a teacher and feed back all that my parents and society had given me through the years. With Doug in full-time Christian work, and with no fixed salary, I could supplement the finances. Juggling home, family and work is managed expertly by men and women in this present day and age, and the pressure was on me to succeed. I spent weeks and months tearing from pillar to post, fulfilling my responsibilities and outwardly appearing to cope. Inwardly, I was losing my grip! Fearing failure, I was sliding into a valley of depression. I lost sight of the people around me and had little time for family and friends. I was approaching Christmas with more money than usual for presents, but no time for the people I was giving them to.

I was stopped in my tracks as the school term accelerated to its close. The word of God is definitely 'sharper than a two-edged sword', because it needed something sharp and forceful to grab my attention. I was sitting in church one Sunday morning, with my mind on the Monday morning lesson I had to take next day. Automatically, I turned to the Bible passage that was being announced in Romans chapter 12. Still with my thoughts elsewhere I followed the words with my eyes until verse two jumped out at me:

Do not conform any longer to the pattern of this world, but be transformed by the renewing of your mind. Then you will be able to test and approve what God's will is – his good, pleasing and perfect will. (Romans 12:2)

My mind had been captured by the motivation of this world, where money, materialism and success are of paramount importance. Teaching, home and family were secondary, and God's will had been ignored in the race to provide for the family and to find self-achievement. God doesn't want us to be irresponsible in our caring for others and ourselves, but he does have a perfect plan for us to test and approve. Just as I needed to test each foothold on my climb of Striding Edge, so I started to examine and test my way ahead with the perspective of my 'all-seeing' guide, God the Holy Spirit. He renews our mind by giving us his perspective, which sees over the craggy edge and round the blind corners. My eventual decision to give up teaching at that particular period of my life released me to give my time, rather than money, to our children. Quality time is a rare and valuable gift in this day and age.

Sinking onto a welcome seat of grey Lakeland rock on the peaceful edge of Red Tarn, Doug and I soaked our weary feet in its cool waters. Having eventually negotiated the descent from the heights, we now lifted our eyes to Striding Edge's twin bony arm towering above us on the other side of the tarn, Swirrel Edge. In the distance, I could just make out the 'specks' of climbers scaling the seemingly vertical rock back to the craggy summit. My stomach started its churning, and memories of childhood fear flooded back.

Taking a last gulp of water, we set out on our return journey home. Owing to fatigue, and ascending rather than descending, I found this a much tougher haul than Striding

Edge. Doug was just ahead of me, and all that was visible of him were the soles of his climbing boots just above me. I didn't dare look down, and focused my mind on testing and eventually pulling myself up on the next foothold. As Doug disappeared over the top, I was momentarily paralysed, clinging to the face of the fell just inches from my face! I reached up to the next rock, which felt insecure in my grasp. There were no other hand- or footholds above, and I could see no way up. I was stuck, and hanging on for dear life! Regaining my breath and steadying my thumping heart, I looked around me in desperation. There wasn't a soul in sight, and I felt abandoned. Suddenly, I heard my name shouted from the summit 30 feet above. I recognised Doug's voice, but couldn't see him from my precarious position. 'Don't climb up that way; edge to your right.' To say I was annoyed was putting it mildly! The sooner I could get to the top, the better. Why did I have to waste time edging to the right and making no progress upwards? Testing the rocks to the right, I found the going much firmer, and several agonising minutes later I crawled, gasping, onto the summit. Having negotiated the path before me, Doug had a much better view and understanding of its pitfalls, and his advice was previously tried and tested.

However super-human we like to think we are, our view of life is limited. God, however, knows the end from the beginning. He sees every step of our human race, and has tested each foothold of the traumatic heights we scale from career crisis to 'parenting paranoia'. Whether we run on the edge, juggling all that life throws at us, just about keeping everything up and running, or whether our experience is the crawling, 'hanging on for dear life' mentality (I alternate between the two) God wants to lead us safely through.

Guide me, O Thou great Jehovah, pilgrim through this barren
  land;
I am weak but Thou art mighty, hold me with Thy powerful
  hand:
Bread of heaven, Bread of heaven, feed me now and evermore,
Feed me now and evermore.

How many times have we heard and sung this hymn to the
famous tune *'Cwm Rhondda'*? William Williams wrote these
words some time between 1717 and 1791, reflecting not only
on the hazards of the Children of Israel's journey through the
wilderness, but those of his own human race and his own
'running on the edge'.

When I tread the verge of Jordan, bid my anxious fears subside;
Death of death, and hell's destruction, land me safe on Canaan's
  side.

As I once more 'trod the verge of Helvellyn' my anxious fears
had subsided, and I looked back the way I had come.

What a difference it makes to know that the God who
'directs proceedings' from above has walked this earth, and,
as fully human, knew every 'edge experience' there is.

... Christ Jesus:
  Who, being in very nature God, did not consider equality with
  God something to be grasped, but made himself nothing, taking the
  very nature of a servant, being made in human likeness. And being
  found in appearance as a man, he humbled himself and became
  obedient to death – even death on a cross! (Philippians 2:5–8)

Try to fathom the depths of despair and the heights of pressure Jesus was treading when he gasped to his disciples in the
Garden of Gethsemane: 'My soul is overwhelmed with

sorrow to the point of death . . . Stay here and keep watch'
(Mark 14:34). When he needed his closest friends the most,
they couldn't even stay awake for him. Does this ring a bell in
your experience? Instead of giving up, Jesus continued to
agonise in prayer. He was fully on the edge of his humanity
and his deity, truly man and truly God, as he cried: ' "Father,
if you are willing, take this cup from me; yet not my will, but
yours be done." . . . And being in anguish, he prayed more
earnestly, and his sweat was like drops of blood falling to
the ground' (Luke 22:42–44). His condition was critical, and
medically his symptoms were the result of extreme mental,
emotional and physical tension. Add to this the major spiritual battle he was fighting, and we discover that the victory of
the cross was won in the Garden of Gethsemane.

With the battle won, Jesus still had to step out of the garden
onto the precipitous path to the cross. He had to face betrayal by
Judas, one of his team of twelve, and denial from Peter, one of
his closer three friends. He was arrested, wrongly accused, and
the roaring of the crowd won the day as they chanted, 'Crucify
him!' Jesus knew every step he had to take to fulfil the victory
won in his mind, heart and will in the Garden of Gethsemane
with his Father. God understands the wars that wage in our
minds that result in 'running on the edge' experiences.

'We still live on the edge of a precipice, and have no confi-
dence in the future.' A gripping article in *The Times* newspaper on mental sickness highlighted the trauma of parents
Marilyn and Alan Lazarus who uttered these words. This
incredible couple have loved and cared for their daughter
Lorraine through 23 years of mental sickness. She has been
severely ill with variously diagnosed personality disorders
including schizophrenia since the age of 17 years. The old idea
of helping people in breakdown by metaphorically 'putting

the mind in a splint', giving time and space for healing, has disappeared. Today, there is a DIY approach – you take the pack of pills and bandage your own nightmares – it's up to you to take responsibility for your illness.

Marilyn and Alan had been told to cut themselves off from their daughter, who has lived in and out of hostels, homes and a police cell. Imagine the agony of a mum's and dad's mind and heart as they had to play back the answerphone message: 'Dad, it's me . . . I don't know what to do. I've gone insane, I need you and Mum badly.'

The final straw came when they were again denied her address after she had been moved by staff to a 'bed and breakfast', following more disruption. Having been part of a therapeutic community, she had been encouraged to stop taking the medication that controlled her condition. Her parents knew only too well the disastrous effects this would have. Hunting high and low for her in the 'B & B' areas of Southhall, they eventually found her, half-naked at the top of a hotel stairway, her entire belongings in a bin-liner. Talking to voices in her head, she was completely unaware that she was seven months pregnant, and desperately in need of medical care.

Living on the edge, Marilyn and Alan have channelled their despair and frustration into helping to raise £1.5 million to build a residential home for mentally ill patients. It is one of the few establishments that provide en suite rooms and no rule to evict guests if they become disturbed. They have fought a case for custody of Lorraine's son, as she is far too disabled to look after him. It is no wonder they find it hard to face the future.

Many of us struggle to understand the precipice of psychological disorder. We can readily appreciate the handicap of a dislocated shoulder, but a dislocated mind and broken heart are hard to grasp, as they are unseen and often only evident through disturbing symptoms and bewildering behaviour.

Having worked with mentally handicapped children, I understand something of the trauma of carers. It was a shock to my system, however, to just briefly experience for myself a disorder to my personal mental attitude and fitness. Visiting Zambia recently, we were prescribed a course of medication to prevent malaria. Lariam is the most successful tablet in protecting against this disease, but also has the strongest side effects if experienced. Depression, we were warned, was one of them. Never having experienced depression, other than feeling 'down' occasionally, I welcomed the weekly tablet in preparation for our trip. Slowly and silently, the effects of this tiny but powerful pill crept through my body to my brain. In contrast to Doug's slight headache on the day of taking the tablet, my whole personality was changed. From being positive, and infuriatingly so at times, I experienced a negativism of frightening proportions. My outgoing nature withdrew into a bewildering tunnel of isolation. I discovered that depression was a complete change of character which distanced me from people and drained me of any point to life. At least for me there was hope after the medication, but I was so low that I wondered whether the tablet had locked in for good! Apart from very occasional recurring symptoms, those days are just a memory. I am thankful now for my wider understanding of the marathon of misery that is run in the minds of so many in this day and age.

The memory of my body's reaction to Lariam returned as I clawed my way up and over Swirrel Edge in the heart of the Lake District. My relief in surfacing from the craggy depths stayed with me on our three mile downhill journey home. How we need to pray for those who are mentally sick, not forgetting those who nurse and care for them.

One of the exercises that helps me focus my mind when training for the marathon is to ask God to protect and keep functioning all the joints, muscles and organs of my body. God urges us to be continually filled with the Holy Spirit (Ephesians 5:18). God the Holy Spirit is often symbolised as oil in the Bible, so what better way of keeping our minds and bodies in good service and working order? Running the marathon has taught me to be intensely specific when asking God to anoint and fill me. When pounding the streets of London, I am aware of the areas that need his attention, and, in time to my running steps, I pray, 'Oil my head, my heart, my hips, my heels.' My childlike mind enjoys alliteration, and this creative praying takes my mind off the pain of the moment and helps a steady rhythm of running.

The J.B. Phillips translation of Romans 12:1 has become a practical and powerful exercise in my human race:

> As an act of intelligent worship, give God your bodies, as a living sacrifice, consecrated to him and acceptable by him . . . Let God remould your minds from within so you may prove in practice that the plan of God for you is good, meets all his demands, and moves towards the goal of maturity.

Stretching exercises

1. Share an experience from your childhood or more recently that stretched you physically beyond what you were used to. Try to describe your emotions and fears at the time.

2. What situations in life cause us to 'run on the edge'?

3. What helps you slow down, and keep perspective, when the going is tough and seemingly endless?

4. Memorise Romans 12:2:

> Do not conform any longer to the pattern of this world, but be transformed by the renewing of your mind. Then you will be able to test and approve what God's will is – his good, pleasing and perfect will.

5. How do you test what is God's will? One example I have found helpful is to write down where I feel God is guiding me, and then date it. With the test of time, God either confirms it through Scripture, other Christians and circumstances, or he allows me to forget it. Pray in twos for God's specific guidance.

LAP 15

Running with the Next Generation

Running to the phone has always been a regular exercise of mine, but it has increased in the past days. August is a good time to be born. It is my month of birth, and many babies seem to be arriving in August this year. I have been on call for two families, in case their expected new arrival makes their entrance at night, and I can be on hand for their siblings. Lauren Grace arrived safely last Tuesday, and now I am secretly hoping my three musketeers, Jo, Ben and Isaac, will need me while Dad and Mum are at the hospital. My tracksuit and trainers are at the ready by the door, and if the phone rings tonight I will literally be running to the call of the next generation. Doug has the car in London, and I must 'leg it'.

These last few days have been an education for me. As I have lain my head on the pillow, my last thought has been, 'Perhaps it will be tonight!' The constant expectation and strong hope has been with me all the time. It seems an age since I gave birth to Stephen and Duncan, but the wonder of new life has grown as the years have gone by. It has now magnified even more since the arrival of our grandson, Morgan.

The question that has challenged me, in these waiting days, is why I haven't the same constant expectation and strong hope for the new birth and life God promises with the coming of his Son. Jesus underlined this promise when he said: 'I have come in order that you might have life – life in all its fullness' (John 10:10 GNB). He was talking to a crowd of living, breathing people. The life that he was referring to is something more than physical life: it makes sense of the human race, and brings the fullness to life with spiritual birth. I will never fully understand this miracle, just as physical birth leaves me speechless, but this doesn't stop me from experiencing both, and longing that others should come into this living relationship with our God and Creator.

Whichever lap we have reached in our human race, there are those around us who need our support and understanding. They too have so much to input into our lives. I have been running alongside five 10- to 14-year-olds in the past two years, who have left me standing at times with their youthful insight. As we welcomed the new millennium in, they welcomed Jesus into their lives. Meeting weekly for keep fit, dance, drama and prayer, their zest for life has motivated me, and their growth spiritually has been evident in the presentations of dance and drama. These lively youngsters have taught me the danger of losing touch with the different generations, both in our family and in the church. We need to be reminded of the Holy Spirit, who continually sweeps round the back of all the age groups. We should follow in his steps, encouraging the 'stragglers', and seeking out those who have lost their way.

One of the biggest learning curves in my human race was

pacing and supporting my parents in the last few laps of their earthly race. They had brought me up in a home that was open to everyone. Mum's nursing and caring welcomed a number of family and friends to spend their last days with us. For my grandmother, Auntie Margaret and a dear old man called Mr Ivymay, the days lasted for years. It was normal family life for us, and I can remember the valuable lessons I learnt from running alongside older, wiser people, as the end to this life was in sight and very real to them.

The trauma of my father dying before her left my mother extremely vulnerable. Osteoporosis had for years crept silently through her body, crumbling bones and leaving her very dependent on my dad. Having nursed so many in her life, she was over-anxious not to burden anyone, knowing firsthand what it entailed. To barge in and take over would not have been the best support, as she hit several walls towards the end of her human race. Bereavement and failing health were major heartaches, but to feel that she was useless and a burden would have finished her. As she had done for so many others down through the years, we welcomed her into our home while she made up her mind about the future. We attended her church every other week, and visited a number of rest homes at her request, to see if she would like to move in. These requests gradually diminished, until one day she said it was time she stayed in our home and church permanently. She had taken a long time to make her final decision, but in retrospect all those months were needed for her adjustment, and reassurance that we really wanted her to come and live with us. I had to adjust my pace of life to her wheelchair and zimmer frame, and had many chats with passers-by as we sat on our halfway wall 'en route' to the shops!

I wouldn't have changed those years. I now understand

that when God slows us down in one area for whatever reason, he accelerates other areas that have been overlooked or neglected because of the pace of life. Running with the older generation developed my listening skills and taught me the powerful exercise of patience and being still. One of the biggest frustrations my mum had was my constant activity. It magnified her disability and feeling of uselessness. As I stopped everything and sat listening to her, or reading with her, the stillness helped both of us.

'Be still, and know that I am God' (Psalm 46:10) is a verse I have always struggled with; I am not a very still person. Since childhood, I have always been on the run – in all senses of the word! In recent years, the discipline of long-distance running has taught me a quietness of spirit that comes through exercise. It releases the stress and tension and renews the mind and perspective on situations. The Good News Bible sheds light on this exercise of 'stillness' with its translation of this verse: 'Stop fighting . . . and know that I am God'. Stress and tension can be magnified when we are supposedly at rest and still, physically. Our minds go into overdrive, and a painful battle ensues. As the nursing of my mother increased, the tension mounted. I would take it out on Doug rather than hurt my mum, and this was affecting our relationship. It was at this time that I discovered the protective power of the name of Jesus, as well as the comfort of his presence.

One of the songs I often find myself singing as I run is based on Proverbs 18:10: 'The name of the Lord is a strong tower; the righteous run to it and are safe.' The steady beat keeps me going and the truth of the words helped me in the tough days of tension to do something physically, which would help me with the spiritual exercise. Just ten minutes' running time away from our home is a large water tower, built high up on

St Catherine's Hill. With this as a goal, I would erupt out of the house, with little time to spare, and escape up the steeper short cut to the tower. I needed the Lord's strength and security to guard my heart, mind *and tongue*. This helped me put my faith into action, and the downhill return always reminded me of the difference our divine Pacemaker has on our run when we stick close to him. Unlike that water tower standing high and out of reach, my 'tower of strength' surrounds me all the time, if only I will accept the fact and trust him.

Returning from a longer run than usual this morning, I took the last turning towards home, joined by the familiar 'whirr' of a motorised wheelchair. As it was slightly behind me, my competitive nature took over and I was determined to stay ahead. My pace automatically increased and my weary legs lengthened their stride. I couldn't believe that at the end of this long stretch of road I was still out front. A few yards from home, a deep voice congratulated me with: 'Well done! You have been running at eight miles an hour. See you again.' This elderly gentleman had purposely stayed just behind me to check my speed – and what a difference he made to that last tough mile. As he disappeared ahead of me, going at an incredible speed, I waved him goodbye and burst into our kitchen with the news of my new fellow runner. He had completely transformed the toughest part of my morning run, and I sat down to work out, from his timing, how fast I could have done the marathon at that speed! Mental arithmetic was never my strongest point, but eventually I discovered that if by some miracle I could keep going at eight miles an hour, I would complete the 26.2 miles in approximately 3 hours 16 minutes and 30 seconds. Never! But it was fun to be motivated for just one mile.

There is a unique view of people from a wheelchair. When trying out a motorised wheelchair for my mother, my father and I took it for a test run. He was hesitant to resort to a wheelchair himself, so I jumped in to set the ball rolling. I was fascinated to observe the reaction of different people to my position. I am thankful I didn't have to stay in it permanently, and was amazed at the change that came when my father had his turn.

Tanni Grey-Thompson comes from Cardiff. She is an incredible athlete, and claimed victory decisively in the London Marathon this year. The eight-time Olympic gold medalist showed why she is one of the greatest British athletes of all time, with a near faultless display in her wheelchair. There was concern at one stage when she suffered from a punctured tyre over the cobbled pathway at the Tower of London, but the Welsh athlete used all her resolve to storm to victory. The determination and perseverance of disabled sportsmen and women can be seen in all generations, and there is so much to learn from them in our human race. After all the goals and medals she has achieved, Tanni still has one more ambition: 'I want to beat Ian, my husband, one day!' Both in wheelchairs, husband and wife, what an historic race that will be!

* * *

Perspiration was pouring off my brow. My arms and legs were aching more than in any other race I had entered. The one thing that was keeping me going was the backside of the lead competitor! He was way out front, and urging us on to catch him. Doug was bringing up the rear, and was fast running out of steam. We had completed numerous laps, and the leader never seemed to tire! In total exhaustion, I collapsed, rolling over on the course with my eyes closed. Doug ground to a halt beside me. We lay motionless, and for a few moments there was silence. Suddenly, we heard a gentle thud from way ahead; it was getting louder – someone was coming to our aid. The heavy breathing became louder, until I felt it on my cheek. A familiar chuckle caused me to open my eyes, and there was the lead 'crawler' himself, our ten-month-old grandson, Morgan. I have never known such energetic baby-sitting, but his mum Sarah has coached him well, and he loves his circuit training. It will not be long before Morgan is walking and running, and I am committed to praying for him, and his dad and mum, every step of the way. Steve and Sarah are a great mum and dad, but parenting is getting tougher as the generations pass, and we should run alongside, not to interfere, but to intercede for them to the greatest parent of all – our Father God.

Stretching exercises

1. Who are you praying for and how do you keep your praying regular, always expecting an answer? (For example, use a prayer diary.)
2. What friends do you have from generations other than yours? What have you learnt from them?
3. How can we practically run alongside those who are older or younger than we are?
4. Are there those in your group who have nursed parents or

friends? Discuss the difficulties and the lessons learnt from these situations.

5. When you experience tension or stress, how do you release it? Discuss ways of dealing with pressure, or avoiding it.

6. Memorise Matthew 11:28: 'Come to me, all you who are weary and burdened, and I will give you rest.' Take this promise with you into your stressful situations and ask God for the rest and peace that only he can give in the most pressurised times.

7. In twos, pray for the people you are really burdened for. If you have photographs of them, it always helps to have a visual aid in prayer. The first scan of Morgan before his birth was a powerful visual aid, and encouraged those who had never prayed in a group before to break the silence.

LAP 16

Keep On Running

The race was on. The runners were lining up. One had his back stubbornly to the course ahead. Another hung on to his dad's hand. One small group were studying the progress of an army of ants in the dirt, while a little lass quietly filled her nappy. All were bewildered by the excitement of the onlookers. 'Ready, steady, go!' resounded round the picturesque quay side, and the cheers of parents and friends echoed into Christchurch. All eyes focused on the mini-runners. The stubborn back continued to face the track ahead. Little hands still clung to legs and trousers. The ant watchers were now sitting in the dirt, following the insects with their fingers, and the nappy was finally full! Suddenly, yards away at the end of the course, came familiar voices: 'Ben! Rees! Maggie! Megan! Run to Mum. Dad's here – get a move on!'

The little bodies turned round in expectation. Heads were raised, eyes lit up, and legs waddled into motion. Crawling, tottering, tripping and straining, they were all making for the finishing line. Not for a prize, but for a person. They saw the face; they knew the voice; they wanted to be with them to feel their arms around them, and to hear the 'well done'.

At whatever stage we are in the human race it is vital that we keep running. Circumstances may bewilder us, crises may cause us to lose direction, but if we keep our eyes focused on Jesus, he will restore our security and will call us in the right direction. The 'coaching tip' in Hebrews 12:2 urges us to 'fix our eyes on Jesus, the author and perfecter of our faith'. There is only one way to run this race successfully, and that is to look to Jesus as our guide and instructor. He created and designed the race, and, as leader and pioneer of it, he must be followed. He has set the course universally and personally, and it makes sense to stick close to him.

Not only has he set the course, but he has also run it, and was the first to finish the race, breaking through the chain of death in victory! Those little faces, as they surged towards their mums and dads in that beginners' race, have stayed with me. Even when they tumbled over, they kept their eyes riveted on that much loved face. Helpers could not distract them. One little fellow dragged himself along the ground with a beaming smile that shone through the dirt, to be whisked up in Dad's arms over the line. Whatever our experience is of an earthly father, we have a heavenly Father who loves us unconditionally and knows what is the very best for us. We must not be distracted from our goal, but must make a deliberate, concerted effort to concentrate on Jesus – not a periodic glance, but a fixed focus. The tumbling toddlers reminded me of the total dependence we have on our parents at this early stage of life. As we mature in the human race, we learn independence, and often the tables are turned as physical life fades and parents become dependent on their children.

This is not so with our heavenly Father. He exists from eternity to eternity. His love is never ending, his strength never fails, and he never has compassion fatigue.

Jeremiah in Lamentations 3 proves this. Here we see a man wrecked by affliction, ageing in darkness and attacked by bitterness. He feels his prayers are not answered, and his heart is broken. The laughing stock of all around, he is mocked and isolated. His running is grinding to a halt, with a loss of hope and peace. The reason why he kept going – and is still teaching us today – is that he dragged his eyes away from the dirt and disaster he was running through, and kept them riveted on the Lord his God. He broke through the wall of adversity, crying: 'Because of the Lord's great love we are not consumed, for his compassions never fail. They are new every morning; great is your faithfulness' (Lamentations 3:22–23).

I remembered this verse just ten days ago, galloping in anger, at the crack of dawn, across St Catherine's Hill. I was consumed with frustration and self-pity. I didn't feel that God cared about my predicament, or why would he have allowed it to happen? I had lost sight of God altogether. The end had been in sight. I had just completed twelve chapters of this book, adding up to approximately 26,000 words. I had been feeling pretty good: tired, but motivated for the last few laps. But I was about to hit the toughest wall in my writing marathon. After three months of capturing thoughts and experiences onto computer, and diligently saving them, I lost all twelve chapters! The document that held 'my book' was completely blank. I was devastated, spending hours through the night searching for it and trying to retrieve it. In desperation, I escaped at first light to the hills to run off the frustration. I cried out to God, who had burdened me with this manuscript since my first marathon. 'Why?' The peacefulness of the countryside heard more than my pounding feet that morning.

God also heard and answered. He reminded me of his promise to the widow of Zarephath in 1 Kings 17:14. All resources had been lost – not through a computer, but through a famine, and she and her son were dying. Through his servant Elijah, God told her to trust him and do what he said: 'This is what the Lord, the God of Israel says: "The jar of flour will not be used up and the jug of oil will not run dry until the Lord gives rain on the land."'

This was all the food she had left for a last meal, and God was promising to multiply it to enable Elijah, her son and herself to survive the deadly famine. God had given me this promise at the outset of my writing. I had been tempted to empty my diary of all commitments to concentrate on writing, but God had other plans. He continually encouraged me to keep running with all he had given me to do, and as I fulfilled my side of the bargain, he would keep the oil of inspiration flowing and the food for thought coming. I had proved this for over three months; now I needed to practise Jeremiah's dogged obedience and faith in trusting God's love, compassion and faithfulness to get me through this obstacle.

Returning home from my long, agonising run, the problem was still there, but my anger had gone. Within an hour, our computer expert and friend Phil had confirmed that somehow I had completely cleared the computer and the disk of all traces of my book! (I learnt the hard way how to save correctly onto a floppy disk!) Seeing my stricken face, he patiently pointed at the printer. 'Have you printed out your chapters?' he enquired. I passed him my file, relieved I had done something right. 'No problem!' was music to my ears, as Phil explained he could scan the chapters onto the computer and disk. Phil saved me on that desperate Saturday morning. It took much patience and time on his part. His wisdom and understanding will not be forgotten.

God has infinite patience with each one of us. He can never be lost, or experience a power cut. He is all seeing, all knowing, and always there. He has all the answers, and the route through any difficulty. His help will never run dry, so we can 'run with perseverance the race marked out for us', fixing our eyes on Jesus.

I was on the edge of my seat, going through the motions of the triple jump at the World Athletic Championships in Edmonton, with thousands of viewers across the world. It was the middle of the night, and the temperature was rising. Jonathon Edwards, having qualified for the final of this demanding and intricate technical discipline, had just flown beyond the 18 metre mark, to be brutally faced with a red flag of disqualification! In the dead of the night, the foundations of our house shook as I lay prostrate before our television, thumping the floor in frustration. In contrast, raising my eyes from my prone position, there was Jonathon quietly pacing back down the track, preparing for his next attempt! How does he keep running, hopping, stepping and jumping through such disappointment and frustration? The secret filters through in his answers in interviews: 'I have gone through six years of intense pressure, and come through it.' This answer suggests that in all marathons of life the route through failure and injury, as well as success, can build in us a strong determination to persevere and succeed. This tour through the tough times led him back down the track to achieve his third round gold medal jump of 17.92 metres. Does this mean Jonathon will compete in the Olympic Games in Athens? His answer to Neil Wilson of the *Daily Mail* has to be an encouragement to us all in the human race. 'I would be 38,' he said. 'If the body is willing, it may be possible . . . There is so much emphasis on age. Once you get to post-30, you are supposed to be grinding to a halt. I have to fight that world-view that past 30 you can't do it any more. Why not? I haven't ruled out Athens, but then I haven't ruled it in . . . It is important to me, but I have two other anchors in my life – my faith and my family. Nothing shakes that, or ever will.' Jonathon has his eyes well and truly open, and firmly fixed on realistic goals.

To keep on running, we must open our ears as well as our eyes. It was hearing their mums' and dads' voices that caused the toddlers at the beginning of the race to raise their heads and start running. We must practise listening up as well as looking up. Samuel would have only been a few years older than our mini-runners when he first heard the Lord's voice (1 Samuel 3). As he is serving in the Temple, he presumes it is Eli the priest calling him. He jumps out of bed and runs to the elderly man's bedside. 'I did not call; go back and lie down,' says Eli. Puzzled, Samuel returns to his bed. The Lord calls him twice more by name, 'Samuel! Samuel!' The third time, Eli realises this must be the Lord speaking to the young lad, and he wisely counsels him: 'Go and lie down, and if he calls you, say, "Speak, Lord, for your servant is listening."'

It is very evident that from this moment on, Samuel was not only on the lookout for his Lord, but he listened carefully for him, too. The evidence lies in the contrast between the first and last verses of 1 Samuel 3: 'In those days the word of the Lord was rare; there were not many visions' (v. 1), and: 'The Lord was with Samuel as he grew up, and he let none of his words fall to the ground . . . The Lord continued to appear at Shiloh, and there he revealed himself to Samuel through his word' (vv. 19–21). Chapter 4 should open with a fanfare of trumpets: 'And Samuel's word came to all Israel.' This is the youngster who didn't recognise the Lord's voice at first, but then, through many years of training, he became the Lord's voice to a nation.

God is calling a people who will listen to his voice and run with his message to our nation. One senses that the days spoken of in Amos 8:11 are true for us today:

> 'The days are coming,' declares the Sovereign Lord, 'when I will send a famine through the land – not a famine of food or a thirst for water, but a famine of hearing the words of the Lord.'

Like Samuel, we need to ask God the Holy Spirit to train us to listen to God's voice. We need to spend more time away from other voices that demand our attention, and, like Jesus himself, withdraw to a quiet place to spend time talking and listening to God.

The main reason why I am still running, ten years after my first marathon, is because I can listen to God far more effectively 'on the run' than when I am still. God has made us all differently, and it is a good exercise to explore the areas and situations that help us focus and listen more easily.

It is a long time since that day I sat on my front doormat, having discovered I had been accepted for my first London Marathon. Many hundreds of miles have been run since then, plus another marathon. If we are to keep running physically, mentally and spiritually we must look ahead and ask God to set our goals. We need to make sure that our goals are his goals. Over the past few months, I have been testing one out by writing this book. As the end is in sight, I reluctantly admit there might be another London Marathon on the horizon. The application forms come out very soon, so thankfully there will be every opportunity for mine to be rejected – or then again, I might be accepted. Help! I'll need some stretching exercises!

Stretching exercises

1. Who has been the 'face' in your human race that has motivated you to keep going? (My games teacher inspired me and was committed to our individual and team success.)
2. Write down or share a circumstance when you felt you lost sight of God. What helped you through?
3. What hinders you hearing God's voice (e.g. media, family)?
4. What helps you listen to God's voice (e.g. music, quietness)?
5. How can we be God's voice to the nation?
6. Share any goals you have, both physical and spiritual.
7. Pray in twos or threes for one another and then for our nation, that the word of the Lord will be heard and obeyed.

Renewing Your Prayer Life

by Sue Barnett

Prayer is about relationships, not rules. Rather than giving a string of formulas for more effective praying, Sue Barnett focuses our attention on the One who both inspires and receives prayer.

This book is for you if

- you are a new believer, keen to develop a more personal relationship with God

- your prayer life is in need of revitalising

'A marvellous challenge! This is not a book one can read passively – it encourages participation.' Fiona Castle

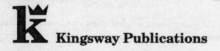

Kingsway Publications